NINETEENTH-CENTURY THEATRICAL MEMOIRS

NINETEENTH-CENTURY THEATRICAL MEMOIRS

Compiled by
Claudia D. Johnson
and
Vernon E. Johnson

GREENWOOD PRESS
WESTPORT, CONNECTICUT • LONDON, ENGLAND

Library of Congress Cataloging in Publication Data

Johnson, Claudia D.
Nineteenth-century theatrical memoirs.

Bibliography: p.
Includes index.
1. Performing arts—Great Britain—Biography—Bibliography. 2. Performing arts—United States—Biography—Bibliography. 3. Theater—Great Britain—History—19th century—Sources—Bibliography. 4. Theater—United States—History—19th century—Sources—Bibliography.
I. Johnson, Vernon E. II. Title.
Z6935.J63 1982 [PN2597] 016.79'02'0922 [B] 82-15576
ISBN 0-313-23644-5 (lib. bdg.)

Library of Congress Catalog Card Number 82-15576
ISBN: 0-313-23644-5

First published in 1982

Greenwood Press
A division of Congressional Information Service, Inc.
88 Post Road West, Westport, Connecticut 06881

Printed in the United States of America

10 9 8 7 6 5 4 3 2 1

Contents

For
Lola Nonnievella Johnson
and
Claudia Haselden Durst

Acknowledgments

For their help in the gathering of information for this bibliography we would like to thank the staffs of the New York Public Library, Harvard University Libraries, the Library of Congress, and the library of the University of Alabama. We also owe a tremendous debt to Lillian Johnson, who helped in the preparation of the index.

Introduction

The definition of the term autobiography assumed for the source work at hand is given by Wayne Shumaker in *English Autobiography* as a Western-world genre of descriptive, narrative, or explanatory tone, which is expected to set out certain of the author's experiences: "ancestry, early life, schooling, young manhood, and an adult career."[1] The modern autobiography, a term used interchangeably with memoir, is a relatively new development beginning in the seventeenth century and taking form in the eighteenth century. Not until the nineteenth century, however, did autobiography in its present shape begin to flourish. A massive new reading public wanted to know more and more about the "real" lives of society's famous and infamous members. At the same time, no group of individuals was as willing to use this relatively new form to entertain the public so readily, consistently, and in such great numbers as were those persons in a variety of branches of show business.

The reasons why this particular group adopted the form is not always apparent in the memoirs themselves, although occasionally writers express hope for monetary return or defend their profession against venomous attack; a few "reformed" actors write to warn readers away from the theatre's temptations. Beyond these expressions of intent, one can only speculate about why the members of a single profession, not ordinarily given to the ritual of religious confession or to the impulse to give practical instruction in worldly success, should so eagerly turn to the writing of their life stories.

The actor, circus manager, or fight promoter knew that even though as individuals they might not enjoy remarkable fame, as professionals they possessed a compelling kind of knowledge. Just as the public clamored for word of remote areas of the globe, it was curious about the equally remote, somewhat scandalous and inverted world called the theatre. Beyond the pale of polite society, show folk made their livings from illusions, painted their faces, slept while respectable people worked, went about their mysterious business at night while ordinary citizens slept, drifted from town to town, and even had a vocabulary all their own. The performer, privy to the exotic rites and colorful personalities of his or her subculture, took the chance that the public wanted a glimpse of this strange world.

In several ways the memoir was an especially suitable literary vehicle for an individual in show business: the written word became an extension of a stage appearance, playing as it did to an audience, necessarily developing a character, even depending for its success on a vogue of personality. Performers, as society's outcasts, may have also felt a special need to justify themselves and to show through autobiography that they wept and bled like other human beings. Furthermore, actors, whose very profession required a public display, were probably less burdened by that false modesty that Ben Franklin saw as an impediment to self disclosure. For whatever reason, hundreds of these memoirs (we have found around 427 extant) were written by show business personalities in the nineteenth century.

It has been our impression that the sheer number of these works suggests that there is a much greater potential here for research than has even begun to be realized. Certainly students of the theatre have for a long time gone to many of the century's prominent autobiographies for firsthand impressions of one of the liveliest periods in stage history, and many of the anecdotes related in the memoirs have long since passed into tradition; information in less familiar memoirs will be found to corroborate and enlarge on what is already known of nineteenth-century entertainments. But in the lesser-known autobiographies one can find information that is not available in the work of stars of the magnitude of Macready, Terry, and Barnum. There are firsthand descriptions of backstage work and estimates of stars from little-known crew members, minor functionaries who were nevertheless professionals. Many of the stories from obscure memoirs reveal a seemingly accurate and ugly side of show business that many other show folk and theatre historians ignore: utter failure, debt, imprisonment, and the exploitation of children. As obviously valuable as this source book should be for theatre historians in particular, we hope that other cultural historians will also find it useful. Here one can uncover a lower layer, something of the humble routines of a multitude of ordinary people, not solely actors: what these individuals ate, how they treated their ailments, how they raised their children, how they travelled, and so forth.

The matter of presenting this source material to the scholar in a useful form is one of the most difficult jobs of the bibliographer. Sooner or later he or she becomes aware of the awesomeness of sitting in supreme judgment over the small world that must be carved out in the course of the endeavor. Though the work is painstaking, it is not trivial, for the lofty task at hand calls for the temerity of a namer, a definer, a discarder, a designer of perimeters—determinations intended but not guaranteed to meet with the approval of all those who come to the bibliography for assistance. In drawing those perimeters, that is in determining what works to include, we have tried to be practical, providing as much breadth as possible without any sacrifice of thoroughness, usefulness, or manageability. Lines have been drawn on several fairly objective bases: form, point of view, chronology, and nationality.

The form of the works included may best and basically be described as the autobiography or personal memoir, a firsthand account of the author's own experience. A few collections of letters and some journals, because they significantly recount events in the writer's life, were judged to belong here. Excluded were fiction, books of craft, nonautobiographical histories written by performers, and biographies of performers written by others.

The memoirs that comprise this bibliography are from the point of view of individuals involved in show business, an extensive variety of people who appeared on theatrical, concert, and variety stages: actors and actresses in the legitimate theatre, strolling players, circus performers, music-hall performers, minstrel men, clowns, acrobats, singers, dancers, magicians, and spiritualists. In the ranks are also those who, while they may not have been visible on stage, were still directly involved in productions in capacities as playwright, manager, producer, costumer, designer, stage-door keeper, agent, or promoter. Some were the most successful people of their day, while others record unrelieved failure. Some made an entire life of the profession; others were actors or managers only briefly. The quality of the memoir and the importance of the career it explores was not found to be a relevant measure for determining its inclusion.

In part because of its extended chronological boundaries, the bibliography at hand greatly supplements James F. Arnott's and James W. Robinson's *English Theatrical Literature, 1559-1900*, which lists only works published up to the twentieth century, thus automatically excluding vasts amounts of information about the last half of the nineteenth century. Our chronological limits were set not by date of publication but by date of subject matter. As a result, an autobiography such as Walford Graham Robinson's *Time Was* is included because Robinson discusses nineteenth-century painters and actors, even though the work was not published until 1931. Any chronological line is somewhat arbitrarily drawn, but limitation based on the time of the subject matter seemed to us to result in a more useful research tool. Such a method provides the theatre historian with sources of extensive material on the fabulous 1880s and 1890s, on the rise of the music hall, the consequences of a long-standing star system, the combination shows, the theatre syndicate, and the changing social status of performers, not to mention a wealth of information on many outstanding stars of the day who were thoroughly identified with the nineteenth century.

Finally, this bibliography embraces the memoirs of those individuals of every nationality who performed in England and America for all or much of their careers. Natives of one country so frequently crossed over to perform and live in the other, that at times it is difficult to distinguish nationality. Indeed, most of the successful theatrical writers had both English and American publishers and readers, as well as English and American careers.

The works are listed alphabetically under the stage name of the author. When available, dates of the author's birth and death are given after his or her name. Names and dates are followed by the full title of the first edition, a description of the work, and short titles of subsequent editions arranged chronologically. The organization of the memoir and the kind of information it furnishes is indicated in the description. From these volumes one expects a variety of material on show business: records of stage personalities, anecdotes, stage traditions, cast lists, playbills, and the details of the often extraordinary day-to-day existence of show folk. The bibliographic description reflects the extent to which such information appears. We also indicate other nontheatrical matters to which the performer's eye frequently turned, such as battles, prisons, exotic countries, and political events.

We designed the Author and Subject Index for diverse uses, but especially to facilitate work in social history. To this end, it incorporates many general topics frequently discussed by autobiographers: the lives of the children of actors, the careers of acting couples, lodging on tour, backstage activity, rehearsal routines, finances, fires and accidents, private clubs, and fashions, to cite a few. A topic is indexed, not when it receives merely a passing mention, but only when it is significantly discussed in a work. Topics are indexed by the number assigned the work in which it is found. Many of the memoirs have their own indices with which scholars may choose to supplement the one provided here.

Below is a selected list of reference works which we found to be of special help in compiling a bibliography of show business memoirs.

Adams, William D. *A Dictionary of the Drama: A Guide to the Plays, Playwrights, Players and Playhouses of the United Kingdom and America From Earliest Times to the Present*. Philadelphia: J. B. Lippincott Co., 1904.

Arnott, James Fullarton, and Robinson, John William. *English Theatrical Literature 1559-1900. A Bibliography Incorporating Robert W. Lowe's A Bibliographical Account of English Theatrical Literature.* London: Society for Theatre Research, 1970.

Baker, Blanche M. *Dramatic Bibliography. An Annotated List of Books on the History and Criticism of the Drama and Stage and on the Allied Arts of the Theatre*. New York: Benjamin Blom, 1968.

______. *Theatre and Allied Arts: A Guide to Books Dealing With the History, Criticism, and Technic of the Drama and Theatre and Related Arts and Crafts*. New York: Benjamin Blom, 1967.

Baker, H. Barton. *History of the London Stage and Its Famous Players (1576-1903)*. London: G. Routledge; New York: E. P. Dutton, 1904.

Baker, Theodore. *Baker's Bibliographical Dictionary of Musicians*. 6th ed. Completely revised by Nicholas S. Lonimsky. London: Collier Macmillan Publishers; New York: Schirmer, 1978.

Blasing, M. K. *The Art of Life*. Austin: University of Texas Press, 1977.

British Museum General Catalogue of Printed Books. 266 vols. London: Trustees of the British Museum, 1965.

Brockett, Oscar G. et al. *A Bibliographical Guide to Research in Speech and Dramatic Art*. Chicago: Scott Foresman and Co., 1963.

Brown, T. Allston. *History of the American Stage*. New York: Dick and Fitzgerald, 1870.

Bruss, Elizabeth W. *Autobiographical Acts*. Baltimore: Johns Hopkins University Press, 1976.

Carlock, Mary Sue. "Writings About the Autobiography: A Bibliography." *Bulletin of Bibliography* 23:118-20.

Clark, Arthur Melville. *Autobiography: Its Genesis and Phases*. Norwood, Pa.: Norwood Editions, 1978.

Connolly, L. W., and Wearing, J. P. *English Drama and Theatre, 1800-1900. A Guide to Information Sources*. Detroit: Gale, 1978.

Cooley, Thomas. *Educated Lives: The Rise of Modern Autobiography in America*. Columbus: Ohio State University Press, 1976.

Couser, G. Thomas. *American Autobiography*. Amherst: University of Massachusetts Press, 1979.

Dictionary of American Biography. Edited by Allen Johnson and Dumas Malone. 7 vols. New York: Charles Scribner's Sons, 1931.

Dictionary of National Biography. Edited by Leslie Stephen and Sidney Lee. 22 vols. London: Oxford University Press, 1949-50.

Donohue, Joseph W. *Character in the English Romantic Age*. Princeton: Princeton University Press, 1970.

______. *Theatre in the Age of Kean*. Oxford: Basil Blackwell, 1975.

Dunn, Waldo Hilary. *English Autobiography*. Folcroft, Pa.: Folcroft Libraries Editions, 1973.

Faxon, Frederick Winthrop. *Dramatic Index for 1909*. Boston: Boston Book Co., 1910.

Gohdes, Clarence. *Literature and Theatre of the States and Regions of the U.S.A., An Historical Bibliography*. Durham: Duke University Press, 1967.

Hartnoll, Phyllis, ed. *Oxford Companion to the Theatre*. 3d. ed. London and New York: Oxford University Press, 1967.

Highfill, Philip H., Jr.; Burnum, Kalman A.; and Langhans, Edward A. *A Bibliographical Dictionary of Actors, Actresses, Musicians, Dancers, Managers and Other Stage Personnel in London, 1600-1800*. 4 vols. Carbondale: Southern Illinois University Press, 1973-.

International Who's Who in Music. New York: Current Literature Publishing Co., 1918.
Kaplan, Louis. *A Bibliography of American Autobiographies*. Madison: University of Wisconsin Press, 1961.
Landow, George P., ed. *Approaches to Victorian Autobiography*. Athens, Ohio: Ohio University Press, 1979.
Loewenberg, Alfred. *The Theatre of the British Isles, Excluding London: A Bibliography*. London: Society for Theatre Research, 1950.
Lowe, Robert E. *A Bibliographical Account of English Theatrical Literature: From the Earliest Times to the Present Day*. London: John C. Nimmo, 1888.
Matthews, Brander, and Hutton, Laurence, eds. *Actors and Actresses of Great Britain and the United States*. 5 vols. New York: Cassell and Co., 1886.
Matthews, William P. *British Autobiographies: An Annotated Bibliography of British Autobiographies Published or Written Before 1951*. Berkeley: University of California Press, 1955.
Mehlman, Jeffrey. *A Structural Study of Autobiography*. Ithaca: Cornell University Press, 1974.
Meserve, Walter J. *American Drama to 1900, A Guide to Information Sources*. Detroit: Gale Research Co., 1980.
Morris, John N. *Versions of the Self*. New York: Basic Books, 1966.
Nagler, A. M. *A Source Book in Theatrical History*. New York: Dover Press, 1952.
National Cyclopedia of American Biography. 56 vols. New York: James T. White, 1898-.
National Union Catalogue. Pre-1956 Imprints. 685 vols. London and Chicago: Mansell Information/Publishing Ltd., 1968.
New York Times Obituaries Index, 1858-1968. New York: New York Times Co., 1970.
Nicoll, Allardyce. *A History of English Drama, 1600-1900*. 6 vols. Cambridge: Cambridge University Press, 1952-59.
Olney, James. *Metaphors of Self*. Princeton: Princeton University Press, 1972.
Oxberry, William. *Oxberry's Dramatic Biography*. 5 vols. London: G. Virtue, 1826-35.
Parker, John. *Who's Who in the Theatre: A Biographical Record of the Contemporary Stage*. 15 vols. London: Sir Isaac Pitman and Sons, 1912-. 16th ed. Edited by Ian Herbert et al. Detroit: Gale Research Co., 1977.
Phillips, Lawrence B. *Dictionary of Biographical Reference*. New rev. ed., 1889. Reprint. Graz, Austria: Akademische Druck, 1966.
Porter, Rosen J. *The Voice Within: Reading and Writing Autobiography*. New York: Knopf, distributed by Random House, 1973.

Russell, Don. *The Wild West: Or, A History of the Wild West Shows.* Fort Worth: Carter Museum of Western Art, 1970.

Saxon, A. H. *The Life and Art of Andrew Ducrow and the Romantic Age of the English Circus.* Hamden, Conn.: Anchor Books, 1978.

Shumaker, Wayne. *English Autobiography, Its Emergence, Materials and Form.* Berkeley: University of California Press, 1954.

Spacks, Patricia Ann Meyer. *Imagining a Self.* Cambridge, Mass.: Harvard University Press, 1972.

Spengemann, William C. *The Forms of Autobiography.* New Haven: Yale University Press, 1980.

Stepto, Robert B. *From Behind the Veil.* Urbana: University of Illinois Press, 1979.

Stott, R. Toole. *Circus and Allied Arts: A World Bibliography, 1500-1957.* Derby: Harpur and Sons, 1958.

Stratman, Carl Joseph. *Bibliography of the American Theatre, Excluding New York City.* Chicago: Loyola University Press, 1965.

Toll, Robert C. *Blacking Up.* New York: Oxford University Press, 1974.

Wearing, J. P. *American and British Theatrical Biography: A Directory.* Metuchen, N.J.: Scarecrow Press, 1979.

______. *The London Stage, 1890-1899: A Calendar of Plays and Players.* Metuchen, N.J.: Scarecrow Press, 1976.

Wethered, Herbert Newton. *The Curious Art of Autobiography, From Benvenuto Cellini to Rudyard Kipling.* Port Washington, New York: Kennikat Press, 1973.

Who's Who in Music and Drama. Edited by Dixie Hines and Harry Prescott. Hanaford, New York: H. P. Hanaford, 1914.

Who's Who in Music and Musician's International Directory. New York: Hafner Publishing Co., 1935.

Who's Who in the Theatre: A Biographical Record of the Contemporary Stage. 1st ed. London: I. Pitman, 1912.

Wilmeth, Don B. *The American Stage to World War I, A Guide to Information Sources* 4. Detroit: Gale Research Co., 1978.

Wilson, Garff B. "Consider Theatrical Biographies." *Yale Theatre Review* 5 (1973): 139-45.

Wyndham, Henry Saxe, and L'Epine, Geoffrey. *Who's Who in Music: A Biographical Record of Contemporary Musicians.* 2d ed. rev. and enl. New York: I. Pitman and Sons, 1915.

NOTE

1. Wayne Shumaker, *English Autobiography, Its Emergence, Materials and Form* (Berkeley: University of California Press, 1954), pp. 4, 28.

Bibliography

A

Anderson, James Robertson, 1811-1895.

1. *An Actor's Life* by James R. Anderson, Tragedian. With an Introduction by W. E. Adams. London: The Walter Scott Publishing Co., 1902. 356 pp.

Although Anderson enjoyed a measure of good fortune in being the protege of Charles William Macready, ill fortune incessantly pursued him. He recounts frequent illness, imprisonment for debt, and disagreements with his managers. In the background of his personal tragedies are violent events on a national scale: the Astor Place Riot, the assassination of Abraham Lincoln, and the attempted assassination of the Duke of Edinburgh. He concludes with an assessment of the low state to which tragic acting has slipped. In addition to this published memoir, Anderson left an unpublished diary, now held by the New York Public Library Theatre Collection, and various memoranda, now in the theatre collection of Harvard University.

Anderson, Mary, 1859-1940.

2. *A Few Memories* by Mary Anderson (De Navarro) London: Osgood, McIlvaine and Co., 1896. 266 pp.

Mary Anderson reflects public attitudes toward the stage and sketches famous painters, writers, generals, and actors she knew. Anderson makes no secret of her own distaste for the theatre, underscoring the ill treatment accorded new-comers to the stage, petty jealousies, and the exhausting physical and mental demands of the profession, all of which she abandons, without hesitation or regret, for marriage.

2a. *A Few Memories* by Mary Anderson. 2nd ed. London: Osgood, McIlvaine and Co., 1896. 266 pp.

2b. *A Few Memories* by Mary Anderson (de Navarro) With Portraits. New York: Harper and Brothers, 1896. 262 pp.

2c. *A Few Memories.* New York: Archer Editions, forthcoming.

3. *A Few More Memories* by Mary Anderson de Navarro. With Seventeen Illustrations. London: Hutchinson and Co., 1936. 286 pp.

This sequel to *A Few Memories* begins with a discussion of Anderson's aversion to her former profession as an actress. She objected to the pretenses so fundamental to acting, as well as to working conditions in the profession. The great joy she takes in her marriage comes, in part, because it enabled her to leave the stage. Beyond the introductory chapter, the memoirs are not theatrical, for Anderson never returned to the stage after she married.

3a. *A Few More Memories* by Mary Anderson de Navarro. London: Hutchinson and Co., 1936. 279 pp.

4. *Girlhood of an Actress* by Mary Anderson. London: Osgood, McIllvaine and Company, 1895. 105 pp.

In the year following its publication, *The Girlhood of an Actress* was encorporated into *A Few More Memories* as the first chapter.

Angelo, Henry, 1760-1839.

5. *Angelo's Picnic: or Table Talk, Including Numerous Recollections of Public Characters Who Have Figured in Some Part or Another in the Stage of Life For the Last Fifty Years* . . . London: J. Ebers, 1834. 400 pp.

As a fencing master and occasional actor, Angelo maintained strong connections to the stage throughout his life. His memoirs contain anecdotes about his and his father's famous fencing pupils, Edmund Kean, Charles Kemble, Jack Bannister, and William Charles Macready.

5a. *Angelo's Picnic* . . . 2nd ed. London: G. Willis, 1840. 400 pp.

6. *Reminiscences of Henry Angelo, With Memories of His Late Father and Friends, Including Numerous Original Anecdotes and Curious Traits of the Most Celebrated Characters That Have Flourished During the Last Eighty Years.* London: Henry Colburn, 1828. 510 pp.

Angelo, who followed his famous father's profession of fencing, writes memoirs primarily of the eighteenth century. However, some judgments are made here of famous actors whom he coached in the early nineteenth century.

6a. *Reminiscences of Henry Angelo . . .* London: H. Colburn, 1828-1830. In two volumes.

6b. *Reminiscences of Henry Angelo . . .* London: H. Colburn and R. Bentley, 1830. In nine volumes.

6c. *Reminiscences of Henry Angelo,* With an Introduction by Lord Howard de Walden and notes and memoir by H. Lavers Smith. Illustrated with Sixty-eight plates, reproduced from originals in the collections of Joseph Grego. London: K. Paul, French, Truber and Co., 1904. Two Volumes.

6d. *Reminiscences of Henry Angelo.* New York: Benjamin Blom, 1969. Two volumes.

Anon.

7. *Letters of an Actress.* New York: Frederick A. Stokes Co., 1902. 325 pp.

> This book, reputedly the letters of an actress named Gladys Luttrell, opens with the editor's claim for the book's authenticity. Though the letters are frequently addressed to actors, the writer records less about the profession than she does about the very personal and social relationships between youthful actors. Even as she records her success on the English stage, she repeatedly professes her weariness with acting.

Anon.

8. *Letters of an Unsuccessful Actor.* London: C. Palmer, 1923. 365 pp.

> In his letters written to a publisher, an unnamed English actor, seemingly old and in ill health, discusses his experiences with many phases of theatre in the late nineteenth and early twentieth centuries: The people involved, the plays, the tone of various theatres, the art of acting, stage business, scenery, and the tenor of the times. He condemns the theatre of the early 1890s for its low taste and poor quality.

8a. *Letters of an Unsuccessful Actor.* Boston: Small, Maynard and Co., 1924. 365 pp.

Anspach, Elizabeth (Margravine of), 1750-1825.

9. *Memoirs of the Margravine of Anspach* Written by Herself. London: Henry Colburn, 1826. Two volumes.

> The Margravine of Anspach, also known as Elizabeth Berkeley Craven, was primarily an eighteenth-century woman of leisure in court society. At the age of thirty-nine she began dabbling in drama by converting a stable into a theatre and producing her own plays.

Brandenburgh House, as the theatre was called, was popular with the aristocracy at the turn of the nineteenth century, but the Margravine's memoirs contain little information about the project.

Archer, Frank, 1845-1917.

10. *An Actor's Notebook, Being Some Memories, Friendships, Criticisms and Experiences of Frank Archer.* London: Stanley Paul and Co., 1901. 345 pp.

Archer's nineteenth-century experiences fall into two major areas. First are his front-line observations of the Franco-Prussian War. Second are his observations of the methods of his fellow performers. Archer affords the reader an unusual record of how individual actors played particular scenes on particular nights.

10a. *An Actor's Notebook* . . . With Forty-Two Illustrations. London: Stanley Paul and Co., 1912. 345 pp.

Arditi, Luigi, 1822-1903.

11. *My Reminiscences* by Luigi Arditi With Numerous Illustrations, Facsimiles, Etc. Edited and Compiled with Introduction and Notes by Baroness von Zedlitz. London: Skeffington and Son, 1896. 352 pp.

Arditi, musician, composer, orchestra leader and opera director, begins his professional reminiscences with his passage to Cuba in 1846 to work with the Havanna Italian Opera Company. Subsequently he worked with other outstanding companies in America, England and Europe, touring the provinces as well as appearing in the major cities. In a career that covered more than half a century, he worked with the greatest names in opera of the time: Madame Alboni, Grisi, Titiens, Adelina Patti, as well as composers Verdi, Gounod, Rossini and Richard Wagner. He characterizes people, evaluates performers and occasionally describes the rigors of performing, particularly on tour.

11a. *My Reminiscences* . . . 2nd ed. London: Skeffington and Son, 1896. 352 pp.

11b. *My Reminiscences* . . . New York: Dodd, Mead and Co., 1896. 314 pp.

11c. *My Reminiscences.* New York: Da Capo Press, 1977. 314 pp.

Arliss, George, 1896-1946.

12. *Up the Years From Bloomsbury. An Autobiography.* Boston: Little, Brown and Co., 1927. 321 pp.

Many of George Arliss' successes were in the twentieth century; however, here he records the nineteenth century experiences which shaped his career: his passionas a child for theatricals, his incurable scene stealing as a "super" in London's Elephant and Castle Theatre, and his gruelling tours in "fit-ups."

12a. *Up the Years From Bloomsbury . . .* New York: Blue Ribbon Books, 1927. 321 pp.

12b. *Up the Years From Bloomsbury . . .* Boston: Little, Brown and Co., 1928. 321 pp.

12c. *On the Stage An Autobiography* by George Arliss. London: John Murray, 1928. 341 pp. An English edition of *Up the Years From Bloomsbury*.

12d. *Up the Years From Bloomsbury . . .* Boston: Little, Brown and Co., 321 pp. 1930.

12e. *Up the Years From Bloomsbury . . .* New York: Blue Ribbon Books, 193_. 321 pp.

12f. *Up the Years From Bloomsbury . . .* Boston: Little, Brown and Co., 1932. 321 pp.

Armfield, Mrs. Maxwell. See Smedley, Constance.

Aronson, Rudolph, 1856-1919.

13. *Theatrical and Musical Memoirs.* New York: McBride, Nast and Co., 1913. 283 pp.

Aronson was an accomplished pianist, violinist and composer who turned his hand to theatrical production. His first major accomplishment was a production in Metropolitan Hall, built at his instigation in 1880. In 1881 he built the New York Casino Company, New York's home for comic opera. Aronson outlines in his memoirs the choices that face a company in designing and constructing a theatre and in hiring performers.

Asche, Oscar, 1871-1936.

14. *Oscar Asche. His Life* By Himself. London: Hurst and Blockett, 1929. 256 pp.

This Australian-born actor, whose real name was John Stanger Heiss, was the black sheep of his family and a runaway. He had what seemed to be phenomenally quick success in breaking into Shakespearean theatre in 1890 in England, learning his craft by playing major character roles in the F. R. Benson Company at Stratford-on-Avon. Benson also prized Asche's skills on the cricket field. Asche's accounts of the Bensonians and their sports and his later association with Beerbohm Tree are told with rare candor and humor.

Ashwell, Lena, 1872-1957.

15. *Myself a Player* by Lena Ashwell. London: Michael Joseph, 1936. 287 pp.

Ashwell knew fame as an actress, manager, and founder of the Lena Ashwell Players. Her memoirs cover her training at the Royal Academy of Music, her apprenticeship as an understudy and her early experiences at the Lyceum Theatre, where she learned stagecraft from Ellen Terry and Henry Irving.

16. *The Stage.* London: Geoffrey Blew, 1929. 192 pp.

Ashwell discusses the changing roles of manager, producers and actors within theatre companies during her life time, the place of theatrical tradition in the mind of the public, the everyday life of the artist, and the relationship of the stage to the nation, the church, and the developing cinema.

Auer, Leopold, 1845-1930.

17. *My Long Life in Music.* New York: Frederick A. Stokes Co., 1928. 337 pp.

Leopold Auer, a Hungarian-born violinist, conductor, and teacher, provides the reader with an intimate view of musical performance in the major cities of Europe. From 1868 until the Russian Revolution, he made St. Petersburg his home. After the revolution, he moved to the United States, but went yearly to England and Europe to participate in music festivals.

17a. *My Long Life in Music.* With Forty-Seven Portraits. London: Duckworth, 1924.

B

Bancroft, George Pleydell, 1868-1956.

18. *Stage and Bar: Recollections of George Pleydell Bancroft* With a Preface by Norman Birkett. London: Faber and Faber, 1939. 343 pp.

> George Pleydell Bancroft, the son of Squire and Marie Wilton Bancroft, was himself an actor for a brief period, then a dramatist, a staff member of Henry Irving's Academy of Dramatic Arts, and clerk of the assize for the Midland Circuit. He describes his childhood, his Eton-and-Oxford education, the theatres and people whom he knew through his parents, and the development of his own dual careers. In large part through his parents, he was able to meet prominent people in the theatre, the law and high society.

Bancroft, Lady Marie. See Bancroft, Sir Squire and Lady Marie.

Bancroft, Sir Squire, 1841-1926.

19. *Empty Chairs* by Squire Bancroft. London: John Murray, 1925. 253 pp.

> Bancroft's chief subjects are the Prince of Wales and other notables in various professions: law, religion, and letters. He reveals the connections between these professions and the stage. His conclusion is a long memorial to his wife, Marie Wilton Bancroft.

19a. *Empty Chairs.* New York: F. A. Stokes, 1925. 253 pp.

Bancroft, Sir Squire, 1841-1926, and Lady Marie Wilton, 1839-1921.

20. *The Bancrofts' Recollections of Sixty Years*: Marie Bancroft, Squire Bancroft . . . With Portraits and Illustrations. London: J. Murray, 1909. 462 pp.

Squire and Marie Bancroft were partners, not only in acting and managing, but in writing (in alternate parts), this their second, highly popular account of professional life. As successful and innovative managers of the Prince of Wales and Haymarket Theatres, they introduced the practice of producing only one play an evening and of preserving the dignity of their actors with decent salaries and working conditions. They pay particular homage to the playwrights who contributed to their success.

20a. *The Bancrofts' Recollections of Sixty Years . . .* New York: E. P. Dutton and Co., 1909. 462 pp.

20b. *The Bancrofts' Recollections of Sixty Years . . .* Popular ed. London: T. Nelson, 1911. 475 pp.

20c. *The Bancrofts' Recollections of Sixty Years . . .* New York: Benjamin Blom, 1969. 462 pp.

21. *Mr. and Mrs. Bancroft On and Off the Stage.* Written by Themselves. With Portraits. London: Richard Bentley and Son, 1888. Two vols.

The most popular of the Bancrofts' several books presents material repeated later in *The Bancrofts' Recollections of Sixty Years* and *Gleanings*, specifically their years in management at the Prince of Wales and the Haymarket theatres. Unlike their other collaborations, this volume is arranged by theatrical seasons. Though the title indicates that the book will cover "off" as well as "on"-stage matters, there is little about their personal lives. For example, no mention is made of their son.

21a. *Mr. and Mrs. Bancroft On and Off the Stage . . .* 2nd ed. London: Richard Bentley and Son, 1888. Two volumes.

21b. *Mr. and Mrs. Bancroft On and Off the Stage . . .* 3rd ed. London: Richard Bentley and Son, 1888. Two volumes.

21c. *Mr. and Mrs. Bancroft On and Off the Stage . . .* 4th ed. London: Richard Bentley and Son, 1888. Two volumes.

21d. *Mr. and Mrs. Bancroft On and Off the Stage . . .* A New Edition Being the 6th. London: Richard Bentley and Son, 1889. 410 pp.

21e. *Mr. and Mrs. Bancroft On and Off the Stage . . .* A New Edition, Being the 8th. London: Richard Bentley and Son, 1891. 410 pp.

21f. *Gleanings from 'On and Off the Stage.'* London: George Routledge and Sons, 1888. 320 pp.

As the title indicates, this volume consists of material selected from *Mr. and Mrs. Bancroft On and Off the Stage,* and appears under Marie Bancroft's name.

21g. *Gleanings from 'On and Off the Stage.'* London: George Routledge and Sons, 1892. 320 pp.

21h. *Gleanings from 'On and Off the Stage.'* London: George Routledge and Sons, 1897. 320 pp.

21i. *Gleanings from 'On and Off the Stage.'* Popular Edition. London: George Routledge and Sons, 1888. 320 pp.

Bandmann, Daniel Edward, 1837-1905.

22. *An Actor's Tour or Seventy Thousand Miles With Shakespeare.* Ed. Barnard Grisby. Boston: Cupples, Upham and Co., 1885. 303 pp.

Bandmann, a German-born actor working in America, conceived the idea in 1879 of making a grand theatrical tour around the world, starting from San Francisco and going to Australia, New Zealand, Tasmania, India, China, the Malay Peninsula and the Hawaiian Islands. In each place, he describes the way of life and the people as well as the theatres. The book emerges as a travelogue with theatrical performances providing the focus. Farms and rural life, convict labor, religious institutions, climate, social conventions and types of government are a few of his topics.

22a. *An Actor's Tour or Seventy Thousand Miles With Shakespeare,* 3rd Revised Edition. New York: Brentano, 1886. 302 pp.

Bantock, Sir Granville, 1868-1946.

23. *Round the World With "A Gaiety Girl"* by Granville Bantock and F. G. Aflalo. London: John Mac Queen, 1896. 171 pp.

Bantock, an English composer, records his 131-day tour around the world in 1894 with a show called "The Gaiety Girl." His descriptions of the American and Australian cities where he toured are detailed and colorful.

Barnabee, Henry Clay, 1833-1917.

24. *Reminiscences of Henry Clay Barnabee: Being an Attempt to Account For His Life, With Some Excuses for His Professional Career.* Ed. George Leon Varney. Boston: Chapple Publishing Co., 1913. 461 pp.

Musical entertainments and the city of Boston in the 1850s and 1860s are the chief subjects of this performer who made light opera his specialty. Also to be found in this memoir are Barnabee's observations of the foreign countries and western territories he toured. A 1908 edition of his reminiscences is included in volumes four and five of *The Scrap Book*.

24a. *Reminiscences of Henry Clay Barnabee*. Ed. George Leon Varney. Freeport, New York: Books for Libraries Press, 1971. 461 pp.

Barnes, Al. G.

25. *Al G. Barnes, Master Showman* by Dave Robeson as Told by Al G. Barnes. Caldwell, Idaho: The Caxton Printers, 1935. 460 pp.

Barnes organized a huge circus which toured the United States and, at his retirement, was sold to John Ringling. The portions of the book dealing with the nineteenth century stress his animal exhibits and animal acts. Included are eighty-six pages of old circus photographs and a lengthy list of "personnel" who worked with him.

25a. *Al G. Barnes . . .* London: J. Cape, 1938. 288 pp.

Barnes, John H., 1850/52-1925.

26. *Forty Years on the Stage; Others (Principally) and Myself* by J. H. Barnes. London: Chapman and Hall, 1914. 320 pp.

J. H. Barnes spent his entire career performing in a variety of theatres in England and America. Unlike most of his successful fellow actors, he never identified with a single theatre for any period in his career. His organization is chronologically arranged around his engagements, and his subject is restricted to his professional life. He worked with and here describes many of the major actors and managers of his day on both sides of the Atlantic. Several nontheatrical matters on which he comments are Mormonism, horseracing and private clubs.

26a. *Forty Years on the Stage; Others (Principally) and Myself*. New York: Dutton, 1915. 320 pp.

Barnum, Phineas Taylor, 1810-1891.

27. *The Life of P. T. Barnum, Written by Himself*. New York, Redfield, 1855. 404 pp.

The 1855 *The Life of P. T. Barnum* includes his youth as a store clerk, his "humbugs" from the time of his first spontaneous performances to his elaborate presentation of the Fee-Gee Mermaid, the opening of the American Museum as a home for "moral" and temperance dramas, and his promotion of Jenny Lind. Until 1869, when he again wrote an autobiography, many excerpts and editions of this book appeared in print.

27a. *Barnum and Money Making; An Autobiography by the Great American Showman, Clerk, Editor, Merchant, and Lecturer. With Rules for Making a Fortune.* London: Willoughby and Co., 185_. 334 pp.

27b. *The Life of P. T. Barnum,* Written by Himself. Author's Edition. London: S. Low, Son and Co., 1855. 404 pp.

27c. *The Life of P. T. Barnum,* Written by Himself. Author's Edition. London: S. Low, 1855. 372 pp.

27d. *The Life of P. T. Barnum,* Author's Edition. London: S. Low, 1855. 246 pp.

27e. *The Autobiography of P. T. Barnum: Clerk, Merchant, Editor and Showman.* London: Ward and Lock, 1855.

27f. *The Autobiography of P. T. Barnum . . . Showman; With His Rules for Business and Making a Fortune.* 5th Edition. London: Ward and Lock, 1855. 160 pp.

27g. *The Life and Adventures of P. T. Barnum, Clerk . . . Showman. With His Rules for Business and Making a Fortune.* 7th Edition. London: Ward and Lock, 1856. 160 pp.

27h. *Barnum on His Feet Again.* New York: no publisher, 1859.

28. *Struggles and Triumphs: or, Forty Years' Recollections of P. T. Barnum.* Written by Himself. Hartford, Burr and Co., 1869. 780 pp.

In 1855 Barnum first published his autobiography. In 1869 he wrote a new life story, identical in subject matter but different in tone. The later book condenses his boyhood years and adds accounts of his loss of a fortune in trying to develop the city of Bridgeport, his recouping of his fortunes, an essay on the art of money getting, his engagement in Civil War matters and post-war politics. The "humbugs" which he had admitted in the earlier volume are now presented as legitimate scientific exhibits, and the moral teaching is more obvious. This autobiography was also frequently reissued in shorter versions, in parts, and with minor additions.

28a. *Struggles and Triumphs . . .* Hartford: Burr and Co., 1870. 780 pp.

28b. *Struggles and Triumphs . . .* Buffalo, Warren and Johnson, 1871. 880 pp.

28c. *Struggles and Triumphs . . .* New York: American News Co., 1871. 856 pp.

28d. *Struggles and Triumphs . . .* Author's Edition. Buffalo, New York: Warren, 1872. 864 pp.

28e. *Struggles and Triumphs . . .* Revised, Enlarged, Newly Illustrated and Written Up to February, 1873, By the Author. Buffalo, New York: Warren, Johnson and Co., 1872. 838 pp.

28f. *Struggles and Triumphs . . .* Author's Edition. Revised . . . and Written Up to February, 1873. Buffalo, New York: Warren Johnson and Co., 1873. 864 pp.

28g. *Struggles and Triumphs . . .* Buffalo, New York: Warren and Co., 1874. 847 pp.

28h. *Struggles and Triumphs . . .* Author's Edition. Revised, Enlarged, and Written Up to March, 1874 By the Author. Buffalo: Warren and Johnson, 1874. 864 pp.

28i. *Struggles and Triumphs . . .* Buffalo, New York: Warren, Johnson and Co., 1874. 870 pp.

28j. *Struggles and Triumphs . . .* Complete to March, 1874. New York: American News Co., 1874. 874 pp.

28k. *Struggles and Triumphs . . .* Written Up to April, 1875 By the Author. Buffalo, New York: Courier Co., 1875. 876 pp.

28l. *Struggles and Triumphs . . .* New York: Arno Press, 1970. 780 pp.

29. *Struggles and Triumphs . . .* Buffalo, New York: Courier Co., Printers, 1876. 314 pp.

> From 1876 a very different edition of *Struggles and Triumphs* appeared. After drastic cutting of the old material and the addition of some new material, the book was now under 400 pages.

29a. *Chapter Fiftieth of Struggles and Triumphs.* Buffalo: no publisher, 1878.

29b. *Struggles and Triumphs . . .* Written Up to December, 1878. Buffalo: Courier Co., 1879. 324 pp.

29c. *Struggles and Triumphs . . .* Revised and Written Up to November, 1879. By Himself. New York: G. Munro, 1879. 52 pp.

29d. *Struggles and Triumphs . . .* Written up to January, 1880. Buffalo, New York: The Courier Co., 1880. 327 pp.

29e. *Struggles and Triumphs . . .* Written Up To December, 1881. Buffalo, New York: The Courier Co., 1882. 758 pp.

29f. *Struggles and Triumphs . . .* Written Up to 1883. Buffalo: Courier Co., 1883. 338 pp.

29g. *Struggles and Triumphs . . .* Buffalo, New York: Courier Co., 1884. 346 pp.

29h. *How I Made Millions; or The Secret of Success.* By P. T. Barnum. Chicago and New York: Belford, Clark and Co., 1884. 355 pp.

29i. *Life of P. T. Barnum . . .* Brought Up to 1885. New York: Hurst and Co., 1885. 357 pp.

29j. *The Story of My Life. A Personal Narrative, Covering a Period of Seventy-five Years (1810-1885), Sixty of Which Were Devoted to a Variety of Colossal, Popular and Successful Enterprises; to Which is Added The Art of Money Getting, or Golden Rules for Money Making.* Cincinnati, Ohio: Forshee and McMakin, 1886.

29k. *The Story of My Life . . .* Boston: B. B. Russell, 1886. Various Pagings.

29l. *The Story of My Life . . .* San Francisco: A. L. Bancroft and Co., 1886. 503 pp.

29m. *Life of P. T. Barnum . . .* Sidney W. Dobell, n.d. 379 pp.

29n. *Life of P. T. Barnum . . .* Brought Up to 1886. Buffalo: Courier Co., 1886. 361 pp.

29o. *Barnum, The Great American Showman . . .* London: J. Diprose, 18__. 80 pp.

29p. *Life of P. T. Barnum Written by Himself, Including His Golden Rules for Money-Making.* Brought Up to 1888. Buffalo: Courier Co., 1888. 357 pp.

29q. *Thirty Years of Hustling or How to Get On.* Rutland, Illinois: C. C. Thompson, 1890. 488 pp.

29r. *Unique Story of a Marvellous Career . . .* n.p., 1891. 621 pp.

29s. *Life of Barnum . . .* Waco, Texas: American Publishing Co., 189_.

29t. *The Life of Barnum . . .* Chicago, Illinois and St. Louis, Missouri: J. H. Chambers and Co., 1891. 450 pp.

29u. *Life of Barnum . . .* London: McDermid and Logan, 1891. 520 pp.

29v. *Barnum, the World-Renowned Showman . . .* Philadelphia, Pa.: 1892. 520 pp.

29w. *The Life of Barnum . . .* Philadelphia: National Publishing Co., 1899. 520 pp.

29x. *Success. The Life of Barnum . . .* Philadelphia: The Book Co., 189_. 500 pp.

29y. *Struggles and Triumphs . . .* New York: The Macmillan Co., 1889. 577 pp.

29z. *Struggles and Triumphs . . .* New York and London: A. A. Knopf, 1927. Two volumes.

29aa. *Struggles and Triumphs . . .* ed. John O'Leary. London: MacGibbon and Kee, 1967. 188 pp.

30. *Barnum's Own Story; The Autobiography of P. T. Barnum,* Combined and Condensed From the Various Editions Published During His Lifetime by Waldo R. Browne. New York: The Viking Press, 1927. 452 pp.

Waldo R. Browne has made a composite of the two autobiographies of Barnum in order to restore the personal and honest tone omitted in the later editions. He also eliminates irrelevant letters, reviews and speeches.

30a. *Here Comes Barnum; P. T. Barnum's Own Story* Collected From His Books and Introduced by Helen Ferris; Illustrated by Franz A. R. Dobias. New York: Harcourt Brace and Co., 1932. 368 pp.

Ferris' book, like Browne's, is a selection from Barnum's two autobiographies.

Barrie, James M., 1860-1937.

31. *The Greenwood Hat, Being a Memoir of James Anon,* 1885-1887. Edinburgh: T. and A. Constable at the University Press, 1930. 315 pp.

The title of this unusual autobiographical book derives from the elderly Barrie's having recovered articles which he had written as a young man for the *St. James Gazette* and which the editor, Greenwood, had published anonymously. Although the book offers little or nothing about the theatre of the period, the feature articles and local color stories, followed by Barrie's comments, provide insight into the growth of a major playwright.

31a. *The Greenwood Hat . . .* author's inscribed presentation copy. London: T. A. Constable at the University Press, 1930. 315 pp.

31b. *The Greenwood Hat . . .* With a Preface by the Earl Baldwin of Bewdley. London: P. Davis, 1937. 285 pp.

Barrington, Rutland, 1853-1922.

32. *Rutland Barrington, A Record of Thirty-Five Years' Experience on the English Stage* by Himself, With a Preface by Sir William S. Gilbert . . . London: Grant Richards, 1908. 270 pp.

Barrington was strongly identified with Gilbert, Sullivan and D'Oyly Carte and his main discussions are of English comic opera in the last decades of the nineteenth century. In addition to portraying theatrical personalities of the times, he describes the elaborate staging of the operas. He also defines and points to the beginnings of musical comedy.

33. *More Rutland Barrington* by himself. London: G. Richards, 1911. 233 pp.

This is a continuation into the early twentieth century of Barrington's first memoirs, developing in greater detail his association with William S. Gilbert. A good portion of the book is devoted to a condemnation of some of the entertainments in the 1890s as immoral and unfit for the children who are allowed to attend them.

Barrymore, Ethel, 1879-1959.

34. *Memories, An Autobiography.* New York: Harpers, 1955. 310 pp.

Ethel, the only one of the Barrymore siblings who had a real love of her profession, describes the life of children in a theatrical household and her own early years on the stage under the sponsorship of her uncle John Drew and, later, Charles Frohman. Not only does she portray her famous family, she also sketches other nineteenth-century figures with whom she worked: Ellen Terry, Henry and Laurence Irving, Mrs. Patrick Campbell and many others.

34a. *Memories . . .* Milwood, New York: Kraus Reprint Co., 1968. 310 pp.

Barrymore, John, 1882-1942.

35. *Confessions of an Actor* by John Barrymore. Indianapolis: The Bobbs-Merrill Co., 1924. 138 pp.

It was not until the twentieth century that John Barrymore very reluctantly gave up a potential career as a painter to become an actor. As the youngest son of one of the most famous theatrical families of the age, however, his account of his formative years is relevant. In the first two chapters of his *Confessions* he writes of his nineteenth century childhood memories--particularly of his grandmother, Mrs. John Drew--and of other actors with whom family associations threw him into contact.

35a. *Confessions of an Actor* . . . London: R. Holden, 1926. 128 pp.

35b. *Confessions of an Actor* . . . New York: Benjamin Blom, 1971. 128 pp.

36. *We Three! Ethel-Lionel-John* by John Barrymore. Illustrations by Courtesy of Metro-Goldwyn-Mayer Pictures. Akron, Ohio and New York: The Saalfield Publishing Co., 1935. 77 pp.

We Three! is an account of the Barrymore-Drew family history and the Barrymore children's first appearance together on stage--in *Camille*. John gives some attention to a portrait of his grandmother, Louisa Lane Drew, his irresponsible father, Maurice Barrymore, and to the three rather pathetic, vagabond Barrymore children.

Barrymore, Lionel, 1878-1954.

37. *We Barrymores* by Lionel Barrymore as told to Cameron Shipp. London: Peter Davies, 1950. 244 pp.

Lionel Barrymore talks of his boyhood in the Drew-Barrymore theatrical family and of his entry, at about fifteen years old, into a profession which he would always find distasteful. He recounts the rise of the theatrical syndicate, the rebellion of such stars as Mrs. Fiske, and the triumph of the Shuberts, for whom Lionel Barrymore worked.

37a. *We Barrymores* . . . New York: Appleton-Century Crofts, 1951. 311 pp.

37b. *We Barrymores* . . . New York: Grosset and Dunlap, 1951. 311 pp.

37c. *We Barrymores* . . . Westport, Conn.: Greenwood Press, 311 pp.

Bates, Helen Marie, 1853-1923.

38. *Lotta's Last Season* by Helen Marie Bates. Limited edition. Privately Printed. Brattleboro, Vermont: E. L. Hildreth, 1940. 306 pp.

Lotta's Last Season is Helen Marie Bates' memoir of her own thirty-weeks' tour in Lotta Crabtree's company in 1889. To this is appended a second part entitled

Shreds and Sketches. Episodes of the Stage of a Bygone Era. Having begun her career as a wardrobe mistress, Bates provides a perspective on theatrical production and backstage life which is rare in the memoirs of actors. In addition, her portrait of Lotta is one of the few close glimpses of an extraordinary performer.

Beale, Thomas Willert, 1831-1894.

39. *The Light of Other Days Seen Through the Wrong End of An Opera Glass* by Willert Beale (Walter Maynard). London: Richard Bentley and Son, 1890. Two Volumes.

Since Beale's father was a musician and manager of the Italian Opera Company, the son grew up knowing music, the theatre and many famous characters. Beale, who followed his father into operatic management, knew and writes about the famous names in opera for two generations. He devotes considerable space to Grisi, Mario, Lord Byron, Count Cavour, and opera at La Scala. He also discusses amateur theatricals, production expenses, gallery behavior, and such unoperatic subjects as a wreck at sea, the siege of Paris in 1870, and spiritualism.

Beatty-Kingston, W., 1837-1900.

40. *Music and Manners, Personal Reminiscences and Sketches of Characters* by W. Beatty-Kingston. London: Chapman and Hall, 1887. Two volumes.

Beatty-Kingston, a librettist, offers the reader little about his own life and career in his "personal" reminiscences. Nevertheless, this two-volume work is a first-hand, highly comprehensive record of several musical communities in different parts of the world from Calcutta to Vienna. He discusses stage design, musical types, music theory and training, the character of audiences and the personalities of performers.

Bedford, Paul John, 1793-1871.

41. *Recollections and Wanderings of Paul Bedford. Facts Not Fancies.* London and New York: Routledge, Warne and Routledge, 1864. 160 pp.

Paul Bedford's memoirs consist of random anecdotes, not always about the theatre or himself, within a framework of his stage experiences which ranged from amateur theatricals to Drury Lane engagements. His fondest memories are of Dublin and his friendship there with Tyrone Power. Bedford concludes his memoirs with a simple list of his friends.

41a. *Recollections and Wanderings of Paul Bedford . . .* London: Strand Printing and Publishing Co., 1867. 132 pp.

41b. *Recollections and Wanderings of Paul Bedford . . .* Another Edition. London: Routledge, Warne and Routledge, 1867. 160 pp.

Belmont, Eleanor Robson.

42. *The Fabric of Memory,* New York: Farrar, Strauss and Cudahy, 1957. 311 pp.

Belmont gives the reader an idea of the home life and expectations in a family of actors in the late nineteenth century. Her own career began at age eighteen in 1897 in the San Francisco Theatre. Before the turn of the century, she had made a tour of Hawaii and, afterwards, had secured a position as an ingenue in a Milwaukee stock company.

Belton, Frederick.

43. *Random Recollections of an Old Actor* by Fred Belton. London: Tinsley Brothers, 1880. 248 pp.

This English actor and manager covers the period of his career from 1815 to 1871; in addition, he characterizes the "old days" and contrasts them with the 1880s in which the book is written. His theatrical subjects include famous entertainers of the period, theatrical agents, amateur theatricals, and command performances at Windsor Castle. Non-theatrical life in London is also part of his discussion: fashion, family life, and the infamous grave robbers, Burke and Hare.

Bennett, Charles Frederick, 1775-

44. *His Memoirs and Poetry* by Charles Frederick Bennett, Second Son of the Late Reverend Thomas Bennett, D.D., Formerly of Trinity-College, Cambridge, and One of His Majesty's Justices of the Peace for the County of Middlesex. Holt: Printed for the Author by J. Shalders, 1817. 144 pp.

This obscure actor got his first taste of theatrics, not from the stage, but in a courtroom as a law student. After his opening in the role of Hamlet in the Norwich Company, he relinquished law for drama and despite his awareness of certain "maladies" of the stage, he strongly defends the profession. Appended to the memoirs is an explanation of the extraordinary circumstances that led to his misfortune, seemingly unrelieved unemployment with the added burden of some ten children who have through mysterious means been left solely in his care.

Bennett, Joseph, 1831-1911.

45. *Forty Years of Music, 1865-1905* by Joseph Bennett. London: Methuen and Co., 1908. 415 pp.

Joseph Bennett, a respected dramatist and librettist, began his close association with the stage as a music critic. His memoirs contain information about light opera in London at mid-nineteenth century. He discusses individuals (Sims Reeves, Erminia Rudersdorff, Charles Halle, Henry John Gauntlett, among others), music journals, grand opera, music festivals, concerts and recitals.

Benson, Constance Samwell, 1860-1946.

46. *Bensonian Memories* by Lady Benson: Introduction by Arthur Machen. London: T. Butterworth, 1926. 313 pp.

Constance Benson, an actress and wife of actor-manager Frank Benson, gives a history of her introduction to the stage and of the Bensonian company of Shakespearean actors formed by her husband. In the course of her history, she pays tribute to every major actor who appeared in the Stratford company.

Benson, Frank Robert, 1858-1939.

47. *My Memoirs.* London: E. Benn, 1930. 322 pp.

About half of Benson's memoirs are of his childhood and Oxford University days. He entered the profession by forming his own theatrical company, whose success was the key to his first engagement at the Lyceum in London. The book is valuable not only for a history of the famous Bensonian Shakespeare Company, but for analyses of the techniques of famous actors. After many successful years with his Stratford-on-Avon Company, Benson followed Henry Irving as manager of the Lyceum.

47a. *My Memoirs.* New York: Benjamin Blom, 1971. 322 pp.

Berkeley, Elizabeth. See Anspach, Margravine of.

Bernard, John, 1756-1828.

48. *Retrospections of America, 1797-1811* by John Bernard. Edited From the Manuscript by Mrs. Bayle Bernard With Introduction, Notes and Index by Laurence Hutton and Brander Matthews . . . New York: Harper and Brothers, 1887. 380 pp.

The last eight chapters of Bernard's *Retrospections* are a history of the development of the American theatre in the early nineteenth century, particularly the mid- eastern circuits. Bernard also writes of the hindrances to the development of the theatre: early church attitudes, Sabbath laws, and municipal fines. Bernard also sets out to characterize different American cities and characters. He knew and wrote about

about Washington, Jefferson and Franklin. He was also particularly interested in the life and character of blacks whom he analyzes, describes and quotes. An earlier volume, *Retrospections of the Stage* stops at 1797 when *Retrospections of America* begins. Some of this material appeared earlier as *Retrospection of the American Stage or Early Days of the American Stage*. London. no publisher, 1884, 1850-51, a fragmentary history of Bernard's American company edited by Laurence Hutton and Brander Matthews and issued in *The Manhattan Magazine* in 1884.

48a. *Retrospections of America* . . . New York: no publisher, 1889. 380 pp.

48b. *Retrospections of America* . . . American Culture Series. Ann Arbor, Michigan: University Microfilms, 1960. 380 pp.

48c. *Retrospections of America* . . . New York: Benjamin Blom, 1969. 380 pp.

49. *Retrospections of the Stage*. By the late John Bernard. London: H. Colburn and R. Bentley, 1830. 2 vols.

Bernard's account covers his childhood until 1797 when he left England for America. After playing Hamlet as a youth and going on a play-seeing tour of London, he ran away to go on the stage, joining "a band of dramatic desperadoes." Woven into his account of life on tour are many anecdotes of nineteenth-century stage stars. An enthusiastic club member, Bernard describes the formation, membership and activities of a number of these gatherings in London.

49a. *Retrospections of the Stage*. Boston: Carter & Hendee, 1832. Two volumes.

Bernhardt, Sarah, 1845-1923.

50. *Memoirs of My Life; Being My Personal, Professional and Social Recollections as Woman and Artist* by Sarah Bernhardt. New York: Appleton and Co., 1907. 456 pp.

Bernhardt had more formal training for the theatre than did many of her English and American counterparts of the day. She recounts something of these years at the Conservatoire and the Comedie Francaise. Of particular interest to the students of Eenglish and American theatres are her conquests of the English-speaking world at a time when her English was so poor that she could scarcely be understood. She expresses the opinions of the American press and show business promoters, a particular obnoxious novelty to which she was introduced in touring the United States.

50a. *My Double Life: Memoirs of Sarah Bernhardt.* London: William Heinemann, 1907. 453 pp. This is an English edition of *Memoirs of My Life.*

50b. *Memoirs of My Life.* New York: D. Appleton, 1908. 456 pp.

50c. *Memoirs of My Life.* New York: D. Appleton, 1923. 456 pp.

50d. *Memoirs of My Life.* Grosse Point, Michigan: Scholarly Press, 1968. 456 pp.

50e. *Memoirs of My Life.* New York: Benjamin Blom, 1968. 456 pp.

50f. *My Double Life.* London: Owen Publishers, 1977. 453 pp.

Berry, William Henry, 1872-1951.

51. *Forty Years in the Limelight* by W. H. (Bill) Berry With a Foreword by Seymour Hicks. With 38 Illustrations. London: Hutchinson and Co., 1939.

> Berry began in the 1890s as a concert hall singer, comedian and manager in establishments like the Chelsea Town Hall, Plymouth Pier and Wellington Pier. Eventually he arrived on the London stage, where his career lasted for thirty years. For twenty of those years he was employed at Daly's and the Adelphi.

Bertram, Charles, 1844-1907.

52. *A Magician in Many Lands* by the Late Charles Bertram With an Introduction by Professor Louis Hoffman. London: George Routledge and Sons; New York: E. P. Dutton and Co., 1911. 315 pp.

> Bertram's memoir is especially useful as a travel book. In his world tours as a magician, he observed the unusual customs of exotic countries, largely unknown to the turn-of-the-century public; he reveals the mystery of the mango trick, the basket trick and other magic of Indian conjurors.

Betterton, Charles, C. 1804.

53. *The Life of Mr. Charles Betterton* Written By Himself. In Two Numbers. Portsea: G. Moxon, 1829. Two Volumes.

> An odd, brief account of a twenty-five-year-old actor who writes facetiously of the beginning of his theatre career. He tells of his attachment to various unnamed members of "the Learned Professions," his dismissal

arising from the seduction of a woman and her two daughters and his life at the Wooden Theatre in Portsmouth in 1828.

53a. *The Life of Mr. Charles Betterton* . . . No. 2. Portsmouth: W. Harrison, 1829.

Bispham, David, 1857-1921.

54. *A Quaker Singer's Recollections* by David Bispham. New York: Macmillan Co., 1920. 401 pp.

Bispham's Quaker parents were unusual in encouraging his attendance at the theatre and his own career as a performer, which began in Philadelphia's amateur societies, drawing rooms and concert halls. After extensive training in Florence, Bispham began his professional singing career at the age of thirty-two in London. He was assured of his success upon receiving a coveted role at the Savoy.

54a. *A Quaker Singer's Recollections* . . . New York: Macmillan Co., 1922. 401 pp.

54b. *A Quaker Singer's Recollections.* New York: Arno Press, 1972. 401 pp.

Blitz, Antonio, 1810-1877.

55. *Fifty Years in the Magic Circle. Being an Account of the Author's Professional Life; His Wonderful Tricks and Feats* by Signor Blitz. Hartford, Conn.: Belknap and Bliss, 1871. 432 pp.

Blitz toured the British Isles, Europe, the United States, Cuba and the West Indies as a ventriloquist and magician. The variety of cultures and classes he encountered in his travels are carefully recorded in his memoirs. He finds a wide range of classes, from Southern slaves to British royalty, worthy of comment.

55a. *Fifty Years in the Magic Circle* . . . San Francisco: A. L. Bancroft and Co., 1871. 432 pp.

55b. *Fifty Years in the Magic Circle* . . . Hartford, Conn.: Belknap and Bliss; Toledo, Ohio: W. E. Bliss, 1872. 432 pp.

Blumenthal, George, 1862-1943.

56. *My Sixty Years in Show Business; A Chronicle of the American Theater, 1874-1934* As Told by George Blumenthal to Arthur H. Menkin. New York: F. C. Osberg, 1936. 336 pp.

Blumenthal went on stage for the first time at age twelve in a Christmas pageant at the Bowery's Stadt Theatre in 1874. At fifteen he began work in the business office of Charles Frohman's Madison Square Theatre and thereafter remained typical of the new businessman who dominated show business at the turn of the twentieth century. Blumenthal was at different times in his life program boy, treasurer, advance agent, manager, and producer. He worked with burlesque, vaudeville, drama, and opera companies.

56a. *My Sixty Years in Show Business* . . . New York: Olympia Publishing Co., 1936. 336 pp.

Bond, Jessie, 1853-1942.

57. *The Life and Reminiscences of Jessie Bond, the Old Savoyard* As Told by Herself to Ethel Macgeorge With Fifteen Illustrations. London: John Lane, 1930. 343 pp.

Jessie Bond, a star for many years with the company of Gilbert and Sullivan, realized at an early age that marriage and a family would not be wise for a star of operettas. She tells the story of a marriage forced on her by a man who intended her to be his support, of her training in church choirs, of the inner workings of the Opera Comique and Savoy Theatres, of her close friendship with Edward, Prince of Wales, and of the hostile attitude of the public toward the theatre.

Booth, Edwin, 1833-1893.

58. *Between Actor and Critic. Selected Letters of Edwin Booth and William Winter.* Princeton, New Jersey: Princeton University Press, 1971. 329 pp.

Although this volume is not strictly classified as an autobiographical memoir, Booth's letters are accounts of himself and his profession in his own words. The letters cover day-to-day details of Booth's management of his New York theatre, the conflict and reconciliation with Lawrence Barrett, and the scandal surrounding his wife's death.

59. *Edwin Booth. Recollections by His Daughter, Edwina Booth Grossman, and Letters to Her and to His Friends.* New York: The Century Company, 1894. 292 pp.

In these letters to his daughter, Edwin Booth tells his own story of life on tour, the receptions he received from different audiences, the sickness and death of Lawrence Barrett, his own last illness and his affection for his daughter. Letters to other friends included in this volume mention the great scandals of his life: his second wife's death and his brother John Wilkes Booth.

59a. *Edwin Booth* . . . New York: Benjamin Blom, 1969. 292 pp.

59b. *Edwin Booth . . .* Freeport, New York: Books for Libraries Press, 1970. 292 pp.

60. *The Last Tragedian. Booth Tells His Own Story* by Otis Skinner. New York: Dodd, Mead and Co., 1939. 213 pp.

Skinner claims that these letters "allow Booth to tell his own story and speak for himself." Included are letters to David Anderson, Richard Henry Stoddard, and Lawrence Barrett. They reveal Booth's grief over the death of his first wife, Mary Devlin, the scandal that his in-laws created over the madness and death of his second wife, and his break with his good friend Lawrence Barrett over a professional misunderstanding.

Booth, Junius Brutus, 1796-1852.

61. *Memoirs of Junius Brutus Booth From His Birth to the Present Time With an Appendix Containing Original Letters From Persons of Rank and Celebrity and Copious Extracts From the Journal Kept by Mr. Booth During His Theatrical Tour of the Continent.* London: Chapple and Co., 1817. 86 pp.

This slim volume contains only one episode in the life of Booth: his memory of a voyage to Holland in 1814. He does, however, provide information on matters both theatrical and non-theatrical: the design of stages, the number and operation of theatres in both Amsterdam and Brussels, and, what particularly struck him about Dutch society, its brutal punishments and executions.

Bostock, Edward Henry, 1858-1940.

62. *Menageries, Circuses and Theatres* by E.H. Bostock... New York: Stokes Publishers, 1928. 305 pp.

Bostock, an English menagerist, circus owner, and producer, began life on the road at the age of twelve when he left school to join the family business. He describes the difficulties of traveling in snow and rain with a collection of animals, the lighting used for his shows, the spectacular accidents that happened in the course of production, and his tours of Australia, South Africa and the Far East. As originator of many variety shows for legitimate theatres, including the Scottish Zoo, the Variety Circus, and the old Olympic Theatre in Glasgow, he was accorded the title, The Barnum of Britain.

62a. *Menageries, Circuses and Theatres.* New York: Benjamin Blom, 1972. 305 pp.

Bowden, George.

63. *The Life and Conversion of George Bowden, Formerly a Player; Wherein is Set Forth the Glory of God's*

Distinguishing Grace, Through the Revelations of Jesus Christ to Him When in Bondage of Soul. Written by Himself For the Glory of God and the Comfort of His Tired People. London: Gold and Walton, 1825. Eight Volumes.

Although Bowden was an actor and had engagements as a boy at Astley's, the Royal Circus and the Royalty Theatre, these volumes contain only four pages about theatrical life. After his conversion, Bowden came to view the players he knew as sinners hungry for applause and money, self-indulgent, lustful and vain.

63a. *The Life and Conversion of George Bowden . . .* Second Edition. London: Palmer and Higham, 1826. Eight Volumes.

Brady, William A., 1863-1950.

64. *Showman* by William A. Brady. New York: E.P. Dutton and Co., 1937. 278 pp.

Brady covers his life and career from childhood in San Francisco and New York, where he worked as a newsboy on the Bowery, to his success as a producer and showman. The book contains a great many vivid details of theatre life of the period, all gleaned from Brady's experiences: his tours of mining towns, his "Tom Shows" and melodramas, his management of James Corbett, the heavy-weight champion, and his notorious lawsuit involving Augustin Daly and Dion Boucicault.

Brookfield, Charles Hallam, 1857-1913.

65. *Random Reminiscences* by Charles H.E. Brookfield. London: E. Arnold, 1902. 305 pp.

The son of a well-known minister chronicles his boyhood. He writes of meeting Garlyle and Tennyson in his childhood home, of schooldays at Westminster, frequent trips to Paris, university life at Cambridge and holidays in the Ardennes. In the account of his success as an actor, he includes anecdotes of Maurice Barrymore, Beerbohm Tree, the Bancrofts and others. He also describes odd character types who haunt stage doors--beggars, swindlers, and "wistful girls."

65a. *Random Reminiscences . . .* 4th Impressions. London: E. Arnold, 1903. 305 pp.

65b. *Random Reminiscences . . .* London: T. Nelson and Sons, 1911. 377 pp.

Brougham, John, 1810-1880.

66. *Life, Stories and Poems of John Brougham . . .* Ed. William Winter. Boston: J. R. Osgood and Co., 1881. 461 pp.

The first ninety-two pages of this volume contain the incomplete "Autobiography of John Brougham," plus fragments of a diary. The autobiography covers his childhood and youth and his early interest in mimicry. The fragments include an outline of his career, his success in America, and a defense of the stage. Among other stories is Brougham's own account of the night on which his play *Pocahontas* was presented without the appearance of the leading character.

Bryant, Billie, 1888-1948.

67. *Children of Ol' Man River; The Life and Times of a Show-Boat Trouper* by Billy Bryant. New York: Lee Furman, 1936. 303 pp.

Bryant's family toured the midwest and southern United States, living marginally as itinerant entertainers for most of Bryant's youth. His father was a medicine man who sold linament and his mother was an enterprising singer and actress. Bryant imitated the act he had seen performed by the boy, George M. Cohan. After much wandering, the family was hired by a showboat company and, at one time, near the close of the nineteenth century, they put together their own dilapidated show-boat.

Buffalo Bill. See Cody, William F.

Bunn, Alfred, 1798-1860.

68. *The Stage: Both Before and Behind the Curtain, From "Observations Taken on the Spot"* By Alfred Bunn, Late Lessee of the Theatres Royal, Drury Lane and Covent Garden. London: Richard Bentley, 1840. Three Volumes.

Bunn, as a very successful theatre manager, encountered and worked with outstanding theatre people, politicians and members of high socity, including Lord Byron, Horace Walpole, Charles Kemble, Sheridan Knowles, Edwin Forrest and many others. In his three-volume memoirs he comments on managment and managers, describes public reactions to amusements, compares rehearsal techniques of the English and French stages and discusses the economic problems involved in running a theatre--all from the point of view of a manager.

68a. *The Stage: Both Before and Behind the Curtain.* Philadelphia: Lea and Blanchard, 1840. Two volumes.

Burke, Billie, 1885-1970.

69. *With A Feather on My Nose* by Billie Burke with Cameron Shipp. New York: Appleton-Century Crofts, 1949. 272 pp.

Burke did not go on stage herself until the twentieth century, but her account of her youth in the nineteenth century as the daughter of a clown sheds light on the unstable family life of many nineteenth-century performers. She describes the times when her father went on extended tours, leaving behind the child, Billie, for years at a time.

69a. *With a Feather on My Nose . . .* London: Theatre Book Club, 1951. 236 pp.

Burnand, Francis Cowley, 1836-1917.

70. *Records and Reminiscences, Personal and General* by Sir Franics. C. Burnand. London: Methuen and Co., 1904. Two volumes.

The first volume is devoted to Burnand's schooling at Eton, where he encountered fagging, and at Cambridge, where he founded the A.D.C., the school's dramatic society. Burnand's conversion to Catholicism, which provoked his father to disown him, made his choice of the theatre an urgent necessity as well as a preference. The second volume of these memoirs is devoted to his career as a writer of plays, chiefly burlesques, for the Royal theatre and an account of his long association with *Punch*.

70a. *Records and Reminiscences . . .* Second edition. London: Methuen and Co., 1904. Two volumes.

70b. *Records and Reminiscences . . .* Third edition. London: Methuen and Co., 1904. Two volumes.

70c. *Records and Reminiscences . . .* Fourth edition. Revised. London: Methuen and Co., 1905. 462 pp.

70d. *Records and Reminiscences . . .* London: Methuen and Co., 1917. 254 pp.

Burton, Percy, 1892-1948.

71. *Adventures Among Immortals* by Percy Burton-Impresario As Told to Lowell Thomas. New York: Dodd, Mead and Co., 1937. 330 pp.

The first three chapters of Burton's autobiography cover three years of the nineteenth century when, as a young boy, he ran away to join Barnum and Bailey's circus. On a tour of England he gained acting experience with Forbes-Robertson and Charles Hawtrey and Learned management from two Americans, Erlanger and Klau.

71a. *Adventures Among Immortals.* London: Hutchinson, 1938. 256 pp.

C

Caine, Hall, 1853-1931.

72. *My Story.* London: William Heinemann, 1908. 398 pp.

Although novelist/playwright Hall Caine writes first of his youth on the Isle of Man and his introduction to literary society, he avows in his introduction that he will submerge his own story in the lives of his friends. His focus is on one friend in particular--Dante Gabriel Rossetti. Caine does write of other friends in the theatre: Wilson Barrett, Henry Irving and Beerbohm Tree.

72a. *My Story.* London: William Heinemann, 1908. 406 pp.

72b. *My Story.* New York: D. Appleton and Co., 1909. 402 pp.

Calhoun, Eleanor, 1862-1957.

73. *Pleasures and Palaces. The Memoirs of Princess Lazarovich-Hrebelianovich.* New York: The Century Co., 1915. 360 pp.

Calhoun was an American-born actress, but the material selected for her memoirs from her journal is about high society in London and in European cities. She has little to offer about the theatre even though some mention is made of her appearances in plays by Sardou, her attendance at performances in Stratford-on-Avon, and her attempts to create a theatre society for the sole purpose of producing classics.

Calve, Emma, 1858-1942.

74. *My Life* by Emma Calve. Translated by Rosamund Gilder. New York and London: D. Appleton and Co., 1922. 279 pp.

Calve's anecdotal memoirs cover her childhood, operatic training, debuts in Brussels and Paris and, in 1893, her debut in New York and tour of the United States. She has special chapters on Adelina Patti, Caruso, Oscar Wilde, gypsies, and Spanish culture.

74a. *My Life.* New York: Arno Press, 1977. 279 pp.

Calvert, Adelaide Biddles, 1837-1921.

75. *Sixty-Eight Years on Stage* By Mrs. Charles Calvert. Ed. Harold Simpson. Illustrated. London: Mills and Born, 1911. 273 pp.

Mrs. Calvert recalls her years as an English actress and wife of actor and Manchester theatre manager, Charles Calvert. She includes scenes of actors' living conditions on tour, detailed accounts of costuming and scene design for individual plays, of managerial problems, and of her associations with designer Alfred Darbyshire, writer Bernard Shaw, and others.

Calvert, Louis, 1859-1923.

76. *Problems of the Actor* by Louis Calvert. With an Introduction by Clayton Hamilton. New York: H. Holt and Co., 1918. 274 pp.

Louis Calvert, son of Mr. and Mrs. Charles Calvert, writes what might more accurately be described as a treatise on the actor's craft than a personal memoir. He uses turning points in his own career to discuss his craft and the meaning of professionalism.

76a. *Problems of the Actor* by Louis Calvert. With an Introduction by Henry Irving. London: Simpkin, Marshall, Hamilton, Kent and Co., 1919. 272 pp.

Cammeyer, Alfred.

77. *My Adventuresome Banjo* by Alfred Cammeyer. London: Cammeyer's, 1934. 335 pp.

Cammeyer, an American-born banjo player, had a classical music education. He moved his residence to England as a young man and took more pleasure in the high society of the 1880s and 1890s than he did in music. His subjects are Queen Victoria, Bond Street, theatrical society, and the homes of the wealthy.

Campbell, Beatrice Cornwallis-West (Mrs. Patrick Campbell), 1865-1940.

78. *My Life and Some Letters* by Mrs. Patrick Campbell. London: Hutchinson and Co., 1922. 359 pp.

Mrs. Campbell describes her unconventional marriage to a military man and the rearing of her children, at the same time that she was actively and successfully pursuing a career on stage. Interspersed with descriptions of her home life, her development of the role of Mrs. Tanqueray, and her friendship with Bernard Shaw, are letters from family members and friends and play reviews.

78a. *My Life and Some Letters . . .* New York: Dodd, Mead and Co., 1922. 451 pp.

78b. *My Life and Some Letters.* New York: Benjamin Blom, 1969. 451 pp.

Capper, Alfred Octavius, 1865-1921.

79. *Rambler's Recollections.* London: G. Allen and Unwin, 1915. 330 pp.

Capper, a thought-reader, made his first London appearances at St. James Hall. His great success led to a command performance before the Prince of Wales. Capper, who maintained close ties with the religious community, writes about prominent clergymen as well as theatrical figures.

79a. *Rambler's Recollections.* New York: Scribner's, 1915. 330 pp.

Carter, Jacob, 1813-

80. *Twenty Years in the Life of a Drunkard From the Year 1825-1845.* New York: Printed by Joseph R. Barr, 1847. 78 pp.

This reformed drunkard claims to have been an inmate of an alms house before he reached his teens. He made his stage debut at the Arch Street Theatre in Philadelphia in 1833, by providing the manager with $225 as "security for the house." He seems to have performed well on tour and, later, with Weymss' Pittsburgh company. He left the stage to join the army only to be thrown out as a drunk. Shortly afterward, he went berserk, dried out, and became a temperance man.

80a. *Twenty Years in the Life of a Drunkard . . .* Boston: Printed by the author, 1847. 96 pp.

80b. *Twenty Years in the Life of a Drunkard . . .* Boston: Printed by the Author, 1848. 96 pp.

Cave, Joseph Arnold, 1823-1912.

81. *A Jubilee of Dramatic Life and Incident* of Joseph A. Cave, Author, Manager, Actor, and Vocalist. Ed. Robert

Soutar. With a Portrait of the Author and of Above Twenty Past and Present Celebrities. London: T. Vernon 1894. 218 pp.

Cave began his career in show business with his appearance as a child in *Tom Thumb*. He served an apprenticeship in utility parts, playing in such establishments as the Apollo Saloon, the Bower Saloon, and the Union Saloon. His range was such that he appeared in both minstrel shows and operas, touring the British Isles and the continent of Europe.

Cellier, Francois, 1850-1914.

82. *Gilbert and Sullivan and Their Operas; With Recollections and Anecdotes of D'Oyly Carte and Famous Savoyards* by Francois Cellier and Cunningham Bridgeman . . . London New York: I. Pitman and Sons, 1914, 443 pp.

Cellier's memoirs are a history of the theatre where he became musical director in 1878. As well as the usual Savoy stories about Gilbert and Sullivan, operas and orchestras, Cellier is a source for the introduction of electric lights to the theatre, the use of the queue system and the conduct of the gallery gods.

82a. *Gilbert and Sullivan* . . . Boston: Little Brown and Co., 1914. 443 pp.

82b. *Gilbert and Sullivan* . . . London and New York: I. Pitman and Sons, 1927. 443 pp.

82c. *Gilbert and Sullivan* . . . New York: Benjamin Blom, 1970. 443 pp.

Chevalier, Albert, 1861-1923.

83. *Before I Forget: The Autobiography of a Chevalier D'Industrie*. London: T. Fisher Unwin, 1902. 258 pp.

Chevalier, famous for his creation of the "cockney coster," recalls his tours of the English provinces and his introduction to American show business. He also indi ates how his songs were marketed and justifies his move from an established career as a comic actor on the legitimate stage to the music hall stage. An index of songs written by or popularized by Chevalier is included.

84. *A Record By Himself*. Biographical and Other Chapters by Brian Daly. London: J. Macqueen, 1895. 295 pp.

Chevalier begins his record when, as a seven-year-old boy, he first went on stage. This, his first memoir, is more anecdotal than *Before I Forget* and includes cast lists and play lists of his provincial tours.

Child Harold, 1869-1945.

85. *A Poor Player. The Story of a Failure* by Harold Child. Cambridge: At-the-University-Press, 1939. 109 pp.

> Child, a highly successful critic and historian, admits to relinquishing his law practice in the 1890s to pursue what turned out to be an unsuccessful career in London and the provinces as a minor actor and understudy. The valuable contacts with successful young couples in London's artistic circles which Child's social status afforded him never lifted him out of his economic and professional poverty as an actor.

Clarence, O.B., 1870-1955.

86. *No Complaints* by O. B. Clarence. With an Introduction by Tyrone Guthrie. London: J. Cape, 1943. 208 pp.

> After a childhood in Ceylon, where his father served on the Supreme Court, Clarence abandoned his original plan to study medicine in order to become an actor. As a character actor in numerous British theatres, including Benson's theatre, he had the opportunity to play a wide variety of roles and to observe many of the most productive performers of his day.

Clarke, Joseph I. C., 1846-1925.

87. *My Life and Memories* by Joseph I. C. Clarke. New York: Dodd, Mead and Co., 1925. 403 pp.

> Clarke, the author of many plays in the nineteenth century, writes about politics, world famous political, scientific and literary characters, and his own promotion of several money-making ventures in entertainment, which included exhibitions, world fairs, grand balls and concerts.

Cochran, Charles Blake, 1873-1951.

88. *I Had Almost Forgotten* by Charles B. Cochran . . . with a Preface by A. P. Herbert. London: Hutchinson and Co., 1932. 304 pp.

> Cochran, an Englishman, worked in both English and American show business as a theatrical agent, manager, vaudeville impresario, private secretary, and producer of rodeos and boxing matches. This is not a continuation of his first book, but instead covers the same material. Although the memoir is primarily about the twentieth century, men and anecdotes of the old days are interspersed throughout.

88a. *I Had Almost Forgotten . . .* Third Impression. London: Hutchinson and Co., 1932. 304 pp.

88b. *I Had Almost Forgotten . . .* Fourth Impression. London: Hutchinson and Co., 1932. 304 pp.

88c. *I Had Almost Forgotten . . .* Fifth Impression. London: Hutchinson and Co., 1932. 304 pp.

89. *The Secrets of a Showman* by Charles B. Cochran. London: W. Heinemann, 1925. 436 pp.

More of an autobiography than his 1932 memoir, this earlier book covers in greater detail Cochran's boyhood, his entry into show business in England, his move to America where times of poverty and failure yielded to success especially in managing, and promoting vaudeville, music halls, rodeos and prize fights.

89a. *The Secrets of a Showman . . .* New York: H. Holt and Co., 1926. 436 pp.

89b. *The Secrets of a Showman . . .* London: W. Heinemann, 1929. 436 pp.

90. *A Showman Looks On* by Charles B. Cochran. London: J. M. Dent and Sons, 1945. 323 pp.

A Showman Looks On covers the twentieth century and only the last decades of the nineteenth century. The early chapters cover nineteenth-century memories of Brighton, the theatre, circuses, clowns, and his introduction to the stage, but reminiscences and anecdotes of the nineteenth century are also scattered throughout the entire volume.

90a. *A Showman Looks On* by Charles B. Cochran. London: J. M. Dent and Sons, 1946. 323 pp.

Cody, William Frederick (Buffalo Bill), 1846-1917.

91. *The Life of Honorable William F. Cody, Known as Buffalo Bill, The Famous Hunter, Scout, and Guide. An Autobiography.* Hartford, Conn.: F. E. Bliss, 1879. 365 pp.

Numerous books purporting to be Cody's autobiography were published over the years, many of them containing much material written by others. As Don Russell has demonstrated, the first edition in 1879 comes closest to being both authentic and truthful. For that reason we are listing that version alone. The last seven chapters deal with Cody's theatrical career up to the year 1879. He appearerd on stage as an actor and also produced, along with Texas Jack Omahundro, the Buffalo Bill Combination, which toured the country, successfully presenting plays, usually melodramas, that starred legitimate actors and actresses as well as such characters as Wild Bill Hickock.

91a. *The Life of Honorable William F. Cody . . .* Foreword by Don Russell. Lincoln and London: University of Nebraska Press, 1978. 365 pp.

Coffin, Charles Hayden, 1862-1935.

92. *Hayden Coffins' Book, Packed with Acts and Facts;* Foreword by the Late Right Honorable T. P. O'Connor, M. P.; Frontispiece by Sir Bernard Partridge; Illustrations by John Hassall. London: A Rivers, 1930. 303 pp.

> Coffin's account is of his career in operas, light operas and musicals, with running commentaries on the people and the shows he was involved with, including his travel in the United States with the Lillian Russell Opera Company. Coffin eventually worked in the movies in the twentieth century.

Cohan, George Michael, 1878-1942.

93. *Twenty Years on Broadway and the Years It Took To Get There: The True Story of a Trouper's Life From the Cradle to the "Closed Shop"* by George M. Cohan. Illustrated. New York and London: Harper and Brothers, Publishers, 1925. 264 pp.

> Cohan, son of traveling American entertainers, was "born in a stage trunk" and entered show business around 1886 when he was eight years old. His cocky scramble for early success as a song-and-dance performer and songwriter in vaudeville was beset with quarrels with managers, agents, publishers, stage-hands and audiences.

93a. *Twenty Years on Broadway . . .* New York and London: Harper and Brothers, Publishers, 1925. American Culture Series. Ann Arbor, Michigan: University Microfilms, 1967. 264 pp.

93b. *Twenty Years on Broadway . . .* Westport, Conn.: Greenwood Press, 1971. 264 pp.

Coleman, George Sanger

94. *The Sanger Story, Being George Sanger Coleman's Story of His Life With His Grandfather, "Lord" George Sanger* by John Lukens. London: Hodder and Stoughton, 1956. 256 pp.

> Grandson of the famous circus showman, George Sanger, and a showman in his own right, George Sanger Coleman graphically portrays the circus as it was for three generations: the machinery required, the design of a circus, production crews, the business of setting up and striking the tents, touring in caravans, and the lives of the circus children.

94a. *The Sanger Story . . .* London and New York: White Lion Publishers, 1974. 256 pp.

Coleman, John, 1831-1904.

95. *Fifty Years of an Actor's Life* by John Coleman, With Sixteen Plates Containing Twenty-Six Portraits . . . London: Hutchinson and Co., 1904. Two Volumes.

> Volume One is an account of Coleman's education in the Catholic Church, his estrangement from his father, and his apprenticeship as a poverty-stricken young actor. Most of the volume is devoted to his appearances in English and Scottish theatrical circuits and in the establshed Glasgow theatres. He provides detailed descriptions of an actor's life on tour--rehearsal routines, lodgings, pawnships, modes of travel--as well as sketches of several notable associates, Charlotte Cushman in particular. Volume Two continues Coleman's account of his early years as a struggling actor and manager. The styles of several actors, including Edmund Kean and William Charles Macready, are examined with candor. Coleman concludes with a plea for a national theatre.

95a. *Fifty Years of an Actor's Life.* New York: Pott and Co., 1904. Two Volumes.

96. *Players and Playwrights I Have Known.* London: Chatto and Windus, 1882. Two Volumes.

> Although this book is made up primarily of lengthy portraits of other actors, the first chapter is devoted to a personal memoir of Coleman's own career. The most extensive portraits are of those actors with whom he worked most closely--the Keans, Macready, Sam Phelps, and Charles Mathews. Volume Two also contains a chapter-long discussion of the social status of actors.

96a. *Players and Playwrights I Have Known.* 2nd ed. Philadelphia: Gebbie and Co., 1890. Two Volumes.

Collins, Horace, 1875-1964.

97. *My Best Riches: the Story of a Stone Rolling Around the World and the Stage* by Horace Collins. London: Eyre and Spottiswoode, 1941. 230 pp.

> Collins is a theatrical business manager whose memories of the nineteenth-century theatre predate his own theatrical career. His first chapters are careful descriptions of the Victorian household of the 1880s and 1890s--its design, its decoration, its family entertainments--in his case, a household which

welcomed entertainers and prepared him and his brothers for careers in the theatre. The nineteenth-century career of one brother, Arthur Collins, who became manager of Drury Lane, is given considerable attention.

Collins, Joe, 1887-1958.

98. *The Maid of the Mountains, Her Story; The Reminiscences of Jose Collins;* With Sixty Illustrations. London: Hutchinson and Co., 1932. 287 pp.

The first two chapters contain nineteenth-century material; Jose Collins did not go on stage until 1900. However, as the daughter of English variety star, Lottie Collins, Jose describes the home life of a traveling performer's children in the 1890s--their unconventional schedules and eccentric visitors, their parents' absences from home, and the preparation of the children themselves for careers in show business.

Conklin, George, 1845-

99. *The Ways of the Circus. Being the Memories and Adventures of George Conklin, Tamer of Lions.* Set down by Harvey W. Root. New York and London: Harper and Brothers, 1921. 309 pp.

George Conklin and both of his brothers worked for the circus for most of their lives. An animal tamer in the last half of the nineteenth century, Conklin records the tours he made by rail and wagon, his animal processions on foot from town to town, a confrontationwith the Ku Klux Klan, a performance on an Indian reservation in the southwest and a visit to Salt Lake City. In addition, Conklin explains each kind of animal he knew and the training methods he used with each.

Corin (pseud. of an actor named Lind), n.d.

100. *Truth About the Stage* by Corin. London: Wyman and Sons, 1885. 180 pp.

After twenty years experience in a variety of theatres, this anonymous actor is compelled to warn his readers about the dangers of the stage to which he had fallen victim. He includes stories about drunkenness, immorality, desecration of the sabbath, extravagance of wardrobe, prostitution, dishonest business dealings, and infamous "green-room suppers."

100a. *Truth About the Stage*. Second Edition. London: Wyman and Sons, 1885. 180 pp.

Cosgrave, Luke, n.d.

101. *Theatre Tonight.* Hollywood, California: House-Warren, 1952. 245 pp.

Born in Ireland during the "troubles," Cosgrave immigrated to America and began his career as an actor in Kansas City. Although his station in minor companies did not provide him with material about important stars of the day, his autobiography is very rich in information about small independent theatre groups on the frontier from New Mexico to Utah in the 1880s and 1890s.

Courtneidge, Robert, 1859-1939.

102. *I Was An Actor Once* by Robert Courtneidge; With Forty-Six Illustrations. London: Hutchinson and Co., 1930. 287 pp.

Courtneidge's greatest financial successes were in theatrical management and playwriting which he turned to in young manhood in order to support his family. He writes graphically of the earlier years as a poverty-stricken actor touring in England and Scotland.

Cowell, Joseph Leathley, 1792-1863.

103. *Thirty Years Passed Among the Players in England and America: Interspersed With Anecdotes and Reminiscences of a Variety of Persons, Directly or Indirectly Connected With the Drama During the Life of Joe Cowell, Comedian.* Written by Himself. In Two parts. New York: Harper and Brothers, 1844. 103 pp.

Cowell recounts his successes as a comedian on the English stage in the early 1800s, his familiarity with the York and Lincoln theatrical circuits, and his admiration for Edmund Kean in particular. Also valuable are his first-hand experiences in a developing American theatre on the frontier where he found engagements as actor and manager in both theatres and circuses.

103a. *Thirty Years Passed Among the Players* . . . New York: Harper and Brothers, 1843. 103pp.

103b. *Thirty Years Passed Among the Players* . . . New York: Harper and Brothers, 1845. 103 pp.

103c. *Thirty Years Passed Among the Players* . . . New York: Harper and Brothers, 1844. American Culture Series 44:3. Ann Arbor, Michigan: University Microfilms, 1956. 103 pp.

103d. *Thirty Years Passed Among the Players* . . . Hamden, Conn.: Archon Books, 1979. 103 pp.

Cowen, Frederick H., 1852-1935.

104. *My Art and My Friends* by Sir Frederick H. Cowen. London: Edward Arnold, 1913. 319 pp.

At nineteen this child of musician parents became an accompanist with Mapleson's Italian Opera Company, a first big step toward his ambition and career as an orchestra conductor and composer. He writes accounts of tours, stars and music festivals throughout the world.

Craig, Edward Gordon, 1872-1966.

105. *Index to the Story of My Days; Some Memoirs of Edward Gordon Craig, 1872-1907.* New York: The Viking Press, 1957. 308 pp.

Gordon Craig was the son of Ellen Terry and the protege of Henry Irving. He first went on stage in 1885 at the age of thirteen. For most of his nineteenth-century years in the theatre, he was an actor and only later, in the twentieth century, turned to stage design and production. In this impressionistically rendered memoir, Craig draws verbal sketches and makes candid judgments about the home life of actors from the point of view of their children. He also stresses the inevitable clash between marriage and profession.

Crane, William Henry, 1845-1928.

106. *Footprints and Echoes* by William H. Crane, With an Introduction by Melville E. Stone. New York: E. P. Dutton, 1927. 232 pp.

Crane was a singer and comedian who enjoyed a long and ultimately successful career from 1863 until the close of the nineteenth century. After a number of years spent touring in English opera companies, he formed a successful partnership in American with Stuart Robson.

Craufurd, Russell.

107. *The Ramblings of An Old Mummer.* London: Greening and Co., 1909. 319 pp.

This actor, who began his career at the Prince of Wales Theatre and traveled throughout the world as an entertainer, was married to an actress in Lydia Thompson's company. A major part of his book is advice to aspiring actors and actresses: he warns them to avoid certain pit-falls and to develop the skills and attitudes required of actors. He also comments on the problems facing the aging actor.

Craven, Elizabeth. See Anspach, Margravine of.

Creswick, William, 1813-1888.

108. *An Autobiography: A Record of Fifty Years of the*

Professional Life of the Late William Creswick. London: James Henderson, 1889. 128 pp.

> Crewick's career was launched in the 1830s when, after some months as an actor's student, he was given the parts of young men in Shakespeare's plays at the Garrick Theatre and the Royal East London theatre. For eight years he worked in stock companies, touring the circuits in England. After seven years in America, he was engaged by Sadler's Wells. Although he enjoyed a reputation as a good actor, his attempts to make money by turning his hand to management were invariably disappointments.

Cushman, Charlotte Saunders, 1816-1876.

109. *Charlotte Cushman: Her Letters and Memories of Her Life.* Ed. Emma Stebbins. Boston: Houghton, Osgood, 1878. 308 pp.

> This kind of memoir, much in evidence in the nineteenth century, consists of Cushman's diary and letters written by her and to her, for which her friend, Emma Stebbins, has provided lengthy transitions. It covers Cushman's apprenticeship in New York, her tour of England, and her triumphant return to America as one of the few members of the profession welcomed into polite society.

109a. *Charlotte Cushman . . .* Boston: Houghton, Osgood; Cambridge: Riverside Press, 1879. 308 pp.

109b. *Charlotte Cushman . . .* Boston: Houghton, Osgood; Cambridge: Riverside Press, 1881. 308 pp.

109c. *Charlotte Cushman . . .* Boston and New York: Houghton, 1899. 308 pp.

109d. *Charlotte Cushman . . .* Boston: Houghton, 1900. 308 pp.

D

Dale, Felix. See Merivale, Herman Charles.

Darbyshire, Alfred, 1839-1908.

110. *An Architect's Experiences: Professional, Artistic, and Theatrical*. By Alfred Darbyshire. Manchester: J. E. Cornish, 1897. 351 pp.

Alfred Darbyshire was an established architect when he was introduced to theatre production in Manchester by actor-manager Charles Calvert. Thereafter, he was absorbed by the theatre and tried his hand at virtually every aspect of stage life: stage design, costume design, theatre design, acting and managing. After Calvert's retirement Darbyshire became more closely associated with Henry Irving's Lyceum and Frank Benson's Shakespeare company. One of the most valuable parts of the book is the account of Darbyshire's attempts to reduce injury and death from fire and panic with more careful theatre design.

111. *The Art of the Victorian Stage; Notes and Recollections* by Alfred Darbyshire. London: Sherratt and Hughes, 1907. 182 pp.

Darbyshire claims that he intends a book of stage craft instead of a personal memoir, and the book's most valuable discussion is certainly its careful description of theatre design for the purpose of prevention of fire and death by fire in the theatre. Nevertheless, the book is a memoir in the sense that Darbyshire writes about his own career and theatrical associates-- Edmund Kean, Samuel Phelps, Henry Irving, and Charles Calvert.

111a. *The Art of the Victorian Stage* . . . New York: Benjamin Blom, 1969. 182 pp.

Dare, Phyllis, 1890-1975.

112. *From School to Stage* by Phyllis Dare. London: Collier and Co., 1907. 146 pp.

This twentieth-century British actress did not make her professional debut until 1900 at the age of ten, but her memoirs include information about child actors and amateur theatricals in the nineteenth century, with a comment on the morals of the green room in the 1890s.

Datas, 1875-

113. *Datas: The Memory Man by Himself.* London: Wright and Brown, 1932. 208 pp.

Datas, an Englishman whose specialty was a show of phenomenal memory, especially for dates, operated on the fringes of the theatre in the late nineteenth century in traveling shows and circuses. He writes in detail about what he knows and what interests him: boxing and boxers, P. T. Barnum and nineteenth-century Australia, where he toured extensively.

Davidge, William Pleater, 1814-1888.

114. *Footlight Flashes* by William Davidge, Comedian. New York: American News Co., 1866. 274 pp.

Davidge provides his readers with one of the most detailed accounts extant of nineteenth-century stage production. He discusses each back-stage position, stage equipment, stock company types, and life on tour. Davidge even provides drawings of mechanical devices used backstage and chemical formulas for special effects. He closes with a defense of the stage.

114a. *Footlight Flashes* by William Davidge, Comedian. New York: American News Co., 1866. American Culture Series 203:4. Ann Arbor, Michigan: University Microfilms, 1962. 274 pp.

Davis, Owen, 1874-1956.

115. *I'd Like To Do It Again* by Owen Davis. New York: Farrar and Rinehart, 1931. 230 pp.

Davis, a successful writer of melodramas at the turn of the twentieth century, describes the state of the drama in the 1880s and 1890s. He compares the actors and directors of this early period to those who rose to prominence thirty years later, and explains the rise of the theatrical syndicate, whose power was eventually broken by the Schuberts.

116. *My First Fifty Years in the Theatre: The Plays, the Players, the Theatrical Managers and the Theatre Itself as One Man Saw Them in the Fifty Years Between 1897 and 1947* by Owen Davis. Boston: Walter H. Baker and Co., 1950. 157 pp.

The first two sections of Owen Davis' autobiography are about the nineteenth century, when he began his career as a mediocre actor and developed into a highly successful writer of melodramas. He explains why his plays were successful at just this time and place and how he went about constructing them. He also discusses the reasons for the decline of the old touring system and the vagabond actor and the rise of the theatrical businessman.

Dawson, James, 1799-1878.

117. *The Autobiography of Mr. James Dawson.* Truro: J. R. Netherton, 1865. 171 pp.

Dawson, who appeared on stage as a boy, was an actor, manager, and dancing master. The book is filled with anecdotes, literary allusions, and philosophizing. Oddly enough, however, except for an account of his boyhood introduction to the stage, he includes little about the theatre.

Day, William C., 1822-1895.

118. *Behind the Footlights; or The Stage As I Knew It.* London: F. Warne and Co., 1885. 191 pp.

Most of the theatre world which William Day knew and wrote about were the amateur theatricals, theatrical societies and theatre clubs. On these subjects he goes into some detail: the typical audiences for which these groups performed, their rehearsal schedules, typical stage design and their use of supernumeraries. Day reveals that he and his associates attempted to bring professional attitudes to amateur theatricals.

De Angelis, Jefferson, 1859-1933.

119. *Vagabond Trouper* by Jefferson De Angelis and Alvin F. Harlow. New York: Harcourt Brace and Co., 1931. 325 pp.

De Angelis, the son of minstrel star, Johnny De Angelis, writes of his childhood among performers in California, his young manhood in tours of the wild west with his family, and, from 1880 to 1884, on a tour of Australia, India, South Africa and the Orient. Details of these exotic places are presented from a performer's point of view. For most of these tours, he and his fellow entertainers were hungry and in poverty, traveling primitively by wagon or on foot, begging lodging and sometimes food.

119a. *Vagabond Trouper . . .* American Culture Series. Ann Arbor, Michigan: University Microfilms, 1967. 325 pp.

Decastro, James, 1758-1835.

120. *The Memoirs of J. Decastro, Comedian. In the Course of Them Will Be Given Anecdotes of Various Eminently Distinguished Characters, With Whom He Has Been Intimate in His Peregrinations . . .* Ed. R. Humphreys. London: Sherwood, Jones and Co., 1824. 279 pp.

Decastro, variously called Jacob, John, Joseph, and James, writes a series of sketches, in third person, of himself and Philip Astley. Much of his story focuses on the Royal Circus and Sadler's Wells theatres. He also includes a collection of rare playbills.

de Frece, Matilda. See Tilley, Vesta.

De Lara, Adelina, 1872-

121. *Finale.* In Collaboration With Clare H-Abrahall. London: Burke Publishing Co., 1955. 222 pp.

Adelina de Lara was one of those unusual, precocious performers whose family used her when she was only a child as a means of support for her mother, father and sisters. As a child of twelve she began touring as a pianist and had a command performance before the Prince of Wales. After being trained by Clara Schumann, she debuted in St. James Hall with great success and later performed at the Crystal Palace and Steinway Hall.

121a. *Finale.* St. Clair Shores, Michigan: Scholarly Press, 1972. 222 pp.

De Lara, Isidore, 1858-1935.

122. *Many Tales of Many Cities.* London: Hutchinson and Co., 1928. 288 pp.

De Lara studied singing and composition at the conservatoir in Milan, taught singing at the Guildhall School in London and earned a reputation as a singer o his own songs. His first opera, *The Light of Asia*, based on Sir Edwin Arnold's book, was produced at Covent Garden in 1892. Many other operas followed: *Amy Robsart, Moina, Messalina* and others. He covers the years of his success in some detail, mentioning his appearances in England, France, Spain and Italy, and his encounters with the great names in opera, the theatre, and high society.

De Mille, Cecil B., 1881-1959.

123. *Autobiography*. Edited by Donald Hayne. Englewood Cliffs, New Jersey: Prentice-Hall, 1959.

In the early chapters of this autobiography De Mille comments significantly on the theatre in the latter part of the nineteenth century and describes his own budding career. Because his father, Henry C. De Mille, was one of the most successful playwrights of his age, Cecil grew up among theatre personalities. He writes perceptive vignettes of such men as Belasco, the Mallory brothers, Charles Frohman and Daniel Frohman. He also writes about his theories of directing and quotes from his father's diary.

De Mott, Josephine, ____-1948.

124. *The Circus Lady* by Josephine De Mott. New York: Thomas Y. Crowell Co., 1926. 304 pp.

Josephine De Mott Robinson, who was reared in a circus, is constantly aware of the circus as an entire world, separate from the outside "real" world of which she knew so little in her childhood. She remembers the trials of traveling by wagon, the summer quarters, and one extraordinary time when she was drugged and married in a scheme by a group of grafters who wanted the profits from her circus act. She later married John Robinson, becoming for a time a politician's housewife, but she could never adjust to or admire the world outside the circus. Finally, after a fifteen-year retirement, she returned to the circus with the full support of her husband.

124a. *The Circus Lady . . .* New York: Thomas Y. Crowell Co., 1936. 304 pp.

124b. *The Circus Lady . . .* New York: Arno Press, 1981.

De Navarro, Mary. See Anderson, Mary.

de Wolfe, Elsie, Lady Mendl, 1865-1950.

125. *After All*. London: Heinemann, 1935. 278 pp.

Elsie de Wolfe opened in New York in Sardou's *Themidor* and subsequently played with John Drew and Forbes-Robertson. Despite a measure of success, she never liked the theatre and retired after about ten years to become an interior decorator and member of the international society set.

125a. *After All*. New York and London: Harper Brothers, 1935. 278 pp.

125b. *After All.* Second Edition. New York: Harper Brothers, 1935. 278 pp.

125c. *After All.* New York: Arno Press, 1974. 278 pp.

Dibden, Charles, the Younger, ca. 1768-1833.

126. *Professional and Literary Memoirs of Charles Dibden the Younger.* Edited from the Original Manuscript by George Speaight. London: Society for Theatre Research, 1956. 175 pp.

Charles Dibden, actor-manager of Sadler's Wells, gives detailed accounts of theatrical management, especially theatre finance, stage design, carpentry, scene painting and costuming. Several unusual entertainments popular in the nineteenth century are described here as well: the theatrical procession, the Aquatic Theatre, and equestrian spectacles.

Dibden, Thomas John, 1771-1841.

127. *The Reminiscences of Thomas Dibden of the Theatres Royal, Covent Garden, Drury Lane, Haymarket, Etc.* Author of the Cabinet, Etc. London: Henry Colburn, 1827. Two Volumes.

Thomas Dibden, the son of Charles Dibden, the first manager of the Royal Circus, began his serious stage career in 1789. By 1800 he was able to secure engagements with Covent Garden. He was to work at a variety of theatrical jobs during his lifetime, most notably as a playwright and as a manager of a number of London theatres. Included in his reminiscences is an exhaustive list of his plays and annual accounts of his expenses and income from acting, writing, and management.

127a. *The Reminiscences of Thomas Dibden* . . . New York: J. and J. Harper, 1828. Two Volumes.

127b. *The Reminiscences of Thomas Dibden* . . . New York: Collin and Hannay, 1828. Two Volumes.

127c. *The Reminiscences of Thomas Dibden* . . . London: Henry Colburn, 1837. Two Volumes.

127d. *The Reminiscences of Thomas Dibden.* New York: AMS Press, 1970. Two Volumes.

Dillon, William A., 1877-1966.

128. *Life Doubles in Brass* by William A. Dillon. Ithaca: The House of Nollid, 1944. 224 pp.

William Dillon, in his boyhood in the 1880s and 1890s, worked in traveling medicine shows as a musician and black-face comedian. He also toured in regular minstrel shows and repertoire theatres. The title indicates the versatility demanded of the performers.

Donaldson, Walter Alexander, 1793-1877.

129. *Fifty Years of an Actor's Life; or, Thespian Gleanings* by W. A. Donaldson, Sen., Professor of Elocution. London: T. H. Lacy, 1858. 56 pp.

Drawing on his own experiences, Donaldson presents brief accounts of certain famous actors of the late eighteenth and early nineteenth centuries, including Edmund Kean, George Frederick Cooke, Michael Kelly, Charles Matthews and Ellen Tree.

130. *Recollections of an Actor* by Walter Donaldson, Comedian. London: John Maxwell and Co., 1865. 360 pp.

Donaldson's recollections are of theatrical tours in Ireland, France and the southern isles of Jersey and Guernsey, all of which he describes in the manner of a tourist's guide book. He tells numerous anecdotes and passes judgment on various actors and managers as individuals and classes.

130a. *Fifty Years of Greenroom Gossip; or Recollections of an Actor.* London: John and Robert Maxwell, 1881. 360 pp.

Douglass, Albert, 1864-1940.

131. *Footlight Reflections: the Musings of One Who Has Spent Sixty Years in the Theatrical Profession* by Albert Douglass. London and New York: Samuel French, 1934. 145 pp.

Although Douglass calls this an autobiography, it is primarily advice to the young actor, manager and amateur theatrical group. Of his own life, we learn little here except that he was born back stage. He is very specific in giving reasons for the failure of theatres and actors and offers them practical ways to correct their deficiencies.

132. *Memories of Mummers and the Old Standard Theatre*: With Illustrations. London: The "Era"; Liverpool: J. A. Thompson; Wallasey: The Winter Gardens, 1924. 138 pp.

Douglass, a member of a theatrical family, was associated with the Old Standard Theatre for around thirty years, rising from call boy to stage manager. He also managed the New Brighton for twenty years. He describes his theatrical family, comments on the sensational melodramas popular during the period, and speculates on reasons for what he sees as the decline of the drama.

132a. *Memories of Mummers . . .* With a Foreword by Lady Mary Wyndham. London: The "Era," 1925. 138 pp.

Dressler, Marie, 1869/71-1934.

133. *The Eminent American Comedienne, Marie Dressler in The Life Story of an Ugly Duckling: An Autobiographical Fragment in Seven Parts; Illustrated With Many Pleasing Scenes From Former Triumphs and From Private Life, Now for the First Time Presented Under the Management of Robert M. McBride.* New York: R. M. McBride, 1924. 234 pp.

Although Dressler did not enjoy success until the twentieth century, her life story contains useful information on the nineteenth century: the north central and New England theatrical circuits she followed, the way in which she broke into the New York theatres in the 1890s, and her work with Lillian Russell, Eddie Foy, and manager A. M. Palmer.

133a. *The Eminent American Comedienne . . .* London: Hutchinson and Co., n.d. 234 pp.

134. *My Own Story* as Told to Mildred Harrington: Foreword by Will Rogers. Boston: Little Brown and Co., 1934. 289 pp.

The second life story of Marie Dressler, written with Mildred Harrington, covers the same ground in the nineteenth century already examined in *The Eminent American Comedienne.* There is very little new information, very little enlargement of the old stories.

134a. *My Own Story . . .* London: Hurst and Blackett, 1935. 256 pp.

Drew, John, 1853-1927.

135. *My Years on the Stage* by John Drew; With a Foreword by Booth Tarkington. New York: E. P. Dutton and Co., 1922. 242 pp.

John Drew, son of John and Louisa Lane Drew, writes about his youth in Philadelphia where his mother managed the Arch Street Theatre. Unlike many actors from theatrical families, John was not put on stage as a child. His is a "professional" autobiography, consisting chiefly of a recital of plays and brief sketches of actors, especially those Drew encountered in his many years with Augustin Daly. The book sheds little light on philosophy, stage craft, history or Drew's own personal life.

Drew, Louisa Lane (Mrs. John Drew), 1820-1897.

136. *Autobiographical Sketch of Mrs. Drew;* With an Introduction By Her Son, John Drew; with Biographical Notes by Douglas Taylor. Illustrated. New York: Charles Scribner's Sons, 1899. 199 pp.

One of the most prominent comediennes and theatrical managers in America, Mrs. Drew tells the story of her stage debut when she was an infant, her move with her actress mother to America and her appearances with the great stars of the American stage. The history of the Arch Street Theatre is very much her own history, although her career continued well into her seventies, after she had relinquished her Philadelphia theatre. There is little information here about her personal life. Three children are accounted for in a one-sentence parenthesis.

136a. *Autobiographical Sketch of Mrs. John Drew . . .* London: Chapman and Hall, 1900. 199 pp.

136b. *Autobiographical Sketch of Mrs. John Drew . . .* New York: Benjamin Blom, 1971. 200 pp.

Duncan, Isadora, 1878-1927.

137. *My Life.* New York: Boni and Liveright, 1927. 359 pp.

The unconventionality of Isadora Duncan is shown not only in her dance, but from her early readings of Ingersoll, and her bohemian life in Chicago, New York, London, Paris, and Munich. In Munich she bore an illegitimate child by Gordan Craig. Even so, she claims to feel a conflict between her art and certain inherited Puritan attitudes. Of particular interest here are descriptions of private entertainments held in the houses of the very rich in London in the 1890s and Duncan's life with Eleanora Duse and Craig in Germany.

137a. *My Life.* New York: Liveright, 1977. 359 pp.

Dunlap, William, 1766-1839.

138. *Diary of William Dunlap (1766-1839). The Memoirs of a Dramatist, Theatrical Manager, Painter, Critic, Novelist and Historian.* New York: Printed for the New York Historical Society, 1930. Three Volumes.

Except for Dunlap's life of George Cooke and his chronology of artists and actors from 1793 to 1832, this portion of his diary yields much less information on the American theatre than one might expect from a pioneer manager. Most of the diary and the letters focus on another of Dunlap's professions--that of portrait painter.

138a. *Diary of William Dunlap . . .* New York: Printed for the New York Historical Society, 1931. Two Volumes.

138b. *Diary of William Dunlap . . .* New York: The New York Historical Society, 1936. Two Volumes.

138c. *Diary of William Dunlap . . .* New York: Benjamin Blom, 1969. Three Volumes in One. 964 pp.

Durang, John, 1786-1822.

139. *The Memoir of John Durang, American Actor, 1785-1816*. Edited and Introduced by Alan S. Downer. Pittsburgh: University of Pittsburgh Press for the Historical Society of Yorke County and the American Society for Theatre Research, 1966.

> Durang began his career at fifteen as a dancer and made his debut in Hallam's Company in 1785. He writes of his experiences in established companies and fit-ups in the Pennsylvania area, discussing social customs, the American Revolution, circuses, tours of Canada and the everyday life of the performer.

Dyer, Robert, n.d.

140. *Nine Years of An Actor's Life*. Robert Dyer, Late of the Theatres Royal, Plymouth, Worcester, Derby, Nottingham, Taunton, Barnstable, Etc., Etc. London: Longman, Rees, Orme, Brown and Co., 1833. 241 pp.

> Dyer was first a comedian, then manager of a traveling company of comedians and, finally, manager of numerous theatres established in England. His comments on actors and their families are extremely candid. From sad experience, he concludes that actors should avoid marriage and parenthood because their children are unable to separate their parents' real characters from the roles the children see them play. After nine years in the profession, he leaves behind the vicissitudes he so graphically describes.

E

Eames, Emma, 1865-1949.

141. *Some Memories and Reflections* by Emma Eames. New York: D. Appleton and Co., 1927. 311 pp.

Emma Eames, a prima donna at the Metropolitan Opera House in the 1890s, was reared in Maine and trained for the stage, first in Boston, then in France and Brussels, and after much adversity, made her debut as Juliet in 1890. Her memoirs describe her friendship with Henry James and the Prince of Wales. She discusses not only opera and fashionable society as she found it in London, but also her often turbulent financial life and her happy home life.

141a. *Some Memories and Reflections.* New York: Arno Press, 1977. 311 pp.

Ebers, John, 1785-1830.

142. *Seven Years of the King's Theatre* by John Ebers. London: W. H. Ainsworth, 1828. 395 pp.

Eber's memoirs, a history of his seven-years' management of the King's Theatre, include extensive records of salaries paid to opera stars and members of the ballet corp, lists of operas selected for presentation, expenses and receipts, number of persons in attendance, number of servants, guards, and other persons employed by the theatre, and backstage accomodations required by opera stars of varying status.

142a. *Seven Years of the King's Theatre.* Philadelphia: Carey, Lea and Carey, 1828. 245 pp.

142b. *Seven Years of the King's Theatre.* New York: Benjamin Blom, 1969. 395 pp.

Ellerslie, Alma, n.d.

143. *The Diary of an Actress or Realities of Stage Life.* Henry Cary Shuttleworth, M.A., Rector of St. Paul's. Griffith, Farron, Okeden and Welsh, 1885. 160 pp.

In this anonymously published memoir, presented in the form of a diary, an actress, identified as Alma Ellerslie, records her thoughts, hopes, disappointments, her rehearsal routine, and her life in provincial companies in residence and on the road. She also reports on the social stigma attached to actresses. Professionally, she never rose above provincial theatres, but she emerges in these memoirs as an engaging and skillful observer of the theatre.

Elliot, William Gerald, 1858-

144. *In My Anecdotage* by William Gerald Elliot. London: P. Allan and Co., 1925. 279 pp.

Elliot's brief stage career, after he finished his Cambridge education, began when Arthur Cecil hired him at the Haymarket in order to encourage other young theatre aspirants at Cambridge to seek theatrical careers. There, at Terry's Theatre in the Strand and the Court Theatre, Elliot played small parts. His career flourished for a time under the managements of Augustin Daly, George Alexander and Cyril Maude before he left the stage.

Ellsler, John Adam, 1821/22-1903.

145. *The Stage Memories of John A. Ellsler, 1822-1886.* Effie Ellsler Weston, Nutley, New Jersey, ca. 1942. 166 pp.

Ellsler chronicles forty-one years spent as actor, barnstormer, producer, manager and theatre builder--a period during which he worked with just about every prominent actor of the period and saw the theatre change from stock company to the combination system. He toured with Junius Brutus Booth, Joe Jefferson, Julia Dean, and many other notables. Much of his career was spent managing theatres in Pittsburg and Cleveland. One of his most revealing portraits is of John Wilkes Booth, whom he regarded a a close friend and business partner and with whom he lived for a time.

145a. *The Stage Memories of John A. Ellsler . . .* Cleveland: The Rowfant Club, 1950. 159 pp.

Elssler, Fanny, 1810-1884.

146. *The Letters and Journals of Fanny Ellsler, Written Before and After Her Operatic Campaign in the United States,*

Including Her Letters From New York, London, Paris, Havanna, Etc. New York: Henry G. Daggers, 1845. 65 pp.

In a series of what she presents as letters written between 1839 and 1842, Elssler comments on her own career in Paris when she was at her peak, her visit to England, her trip to America where she appeared at the Park Theatre with great success, and a journey to Havanna. The letters are long and journalistic; she discusses French and German critics, the London theatre, details of her sea voyages, and gives lengthy descriptions of New York and Cuba.

Ely, Sally Frothingham, 1873-1917.

147. *A Singer's Story.* Stanford: The University Press of Stanford University, 19--. 151 pp.

Frothingham writes about her youth, her portrait painter father, and her own training as a singer with Madame Marchesi. Frothingham developed tuberculosis while she was a student. Not long after her first public recital and despite the promise of her career, she relinquished her profession for marriage.

Everard, Edward Cape, 1755-

148. *Memoirs of an Unfortunate Son of Thespis; Being a Sketch of the Life of Edward Cape Everard, Comedian, Twenty-Three Years of the Theatre-Royal, Drury-Lane, London, and Pupil of the Late David Garrick, Esq.* With Reflections, Remarks, and Anecdotes, Written By Himself. Edinburgh: James Ballantyne and Co., 1818. 274 pp.

Everard's professional life consisted of an often-repeated melancholy pattern: traveling from town to town, renting theatres or suitable space in hotels and taverns for the presentation of readings or dancing exhibitions, and supplementing his meagre income by tutoring and writing, especially for attorneys. He writes these memoirs, seemingly in penury, to procure "a bit of bread for myself and wife." As a picture of life eked out by hundreds of professionals who never became stars, these memoirs are exceedingly valuable.

Eytinge, Rose, 1835-1911.

149. *The Memories of Rose Eytinge; Being Recollections of Men, Women, and Events During Half a Century* by Rose Eytinge. New York: F. A. Stokes and Co., 1905. 311 pp.

Etyinge's career was closely tied to managers Lester Wallack, James W. Wallack, E. L. Davenport, and A. M. Palmer. Not only does she comment extensively on the

New York stage figures whom she knew, but on her reactions to non-theatrical matters: the Civil War, Lincoln's assassination, a trip she made to Egypt, where she became interested in the status of that country's women, and a tour she made of the American west, which included mining towns and Salt Lake City.

F

Fagan, Elizabeth, n.d.

150. *From the Wings, By "The Stage Cat."* Ed. Elizabeth Fagan. London: W. Collins Sons, 1922. 239 pp.

Fagan, an English actress, studied acting under Dame Genevieve Ward, secured her first job with Lewis Waller and A. M. Morell, and worked with the Benson Company. In addition to sketching fellow performers, she comments briefly on one-night stands, "matinee idols," morality and stage life, and lodgings on tour.

Fairbrother, Sydney, 1872-1941.

151. *Through An Old Stage Door*; With an Appreciation by Sydney Carroll, and an Introduction by Stephen Gwynn. London: F. Muller, 1939. 255 pp.

Sydney Fairbrother, the granddaughter of Joe Cowell, was reared in a theatrical family and married to an actor. She went on stage as a juvenile performer and worked in several companies, including that of her step-father, touring both England and America. She met with the greatest success as a comedian. Her memoirs reveal the point of view of an individual whose life from beginning to end is spent in the theatre among performers.

Fay, William George, 1872-1949.

152. *The Fays of the Abbey Theatre. An Autobiographical Record* by W. G. Fay and Catherine Carswell. London: Rich and Cowan, 1935. 313 pp.

Fay describes his youthful participation in amateur theatricals in Ireland, the touring entertainments and drama schools, all of which prepared him for his part in the organization of Dublin's Abbey Theatre. His descriptions of the chores of an advance agent and the life of an actor in "fit-ups" are particularly valuable.

152a. *The Fays of the Abbey Theatre.* New York: Harcourt Brace and Co., 1935. 313 pp.

152b. *The Fays of the Abbey Theatre.* New York: Benjamin Blom, 1971. 313 pp.

Fellows, Dexter, 1871-1937.

153. *This Way To The Big Show; The Life of Dexter Fellows* by Dexter Fellows and Andrew A. Freeman. New York: The Viking Press, 1936. 352 pp.

Fellows, an American press agent for circuses for forty-three years, worked for Buffalo Bill's Wild West Show and P. T. Barnum's circus. He details the make-up of the Cody organization that included Sitting Bull, Chief Joseph, Johnny Baker, Frank Butler and others. He describes the show's progress and relates many anecdotes. An appendix contains portions of a diary for the year 1896, kept by M. B. Bailey, superintendent of lights for the Wild West show, recording graphically the daily life, the hardships, the competition, and the schedules of the troupe.

Fennell, James, 1766-1816.

154. *An Apology for the Life of James Fennell* by Himself. Philadelphia: Moses Thomas, 1814. 510 pp.

Fennell was born in 1766, educated at Eton, and supported by his father in his initial ventures in his profession. Moving to America, he worked with theatrical pioneers--Wignall, Reinagle and the Merrys--playing primarily in Philadelphia, Baltimore and Boston. His exceptional memoirs contain sociological observations on conditions of the poor, the family, and women. Unrelieved poverty, a crippling accident and constant quarrels with managers finally drove him from the profession. He concludes with comments on novel reading, education, lawyers and the stage.

154a. *An Apology for the Life of James Fennell.* New York: Benjamin Blom, 1969. 510 pp.

Field, Alfred Griffith, 1852-1921.

155. *Watch Yourself Go By*, A Book By Al G. Field. Columbus, Ohio: Spohr and Glenn, 1912. 593 pp.

Field was an American singer, minstrel man and producer, who also did circus work. He is best known as owner of A. G. Field Minstrels. The book contains a long, detailed account of his childhood, family and friends, followed by his subsequent success with his own company.

Fields, W. C., 1879/80-1946.

156. *W. C. Fields By Himself; His Intended Autobiography.* Commentary by Ronald J. Fields. Englewood Cliffs, New Jersey: Prentice-Hall, 1973. 510 pp.

Only the first chapter of these memoirs, compiled from unfinished notes for an autobiography, are pertinent to the nineteenth century. However, the author does tell his readers what it was like, in the last years of the century, for a young man to attempt to break into show business by playing concessions, carnivals and vaudeville as a juggler.

Fisher, Clara. See Maeder, Clara Fisher.

Fitch, Clyde, 1865-1909.

157. *Clyde Fitch and His Letters.* Ed. Montrose J. Moses and Virginia Gerson. Boston: Little, Brown and Co., 1924. 386 pp.

These letters, written between the years 1884 and 1909, serve the purpose of memoirs in that Fitch records in them his childhood, his education at Amherst, and the beginning of his career in the theatre. Fitch comments in some detail on his quarrels with the press, his skill at presenting his own work, and the changes which took place in the theatre during the 1980s. The editors have included a list of his plays along with the dates, places, and casts of original performances.

Fitzball, Edward, 1792-1873.

158. *Thirty-Five Years of a Dramatic Author's Life* by Edward Fitzball, Esq. London: T.C. Newby, 1859. Two Vols. in One.

When he was about nineteen years old, Fitzball left home for a printing job and met with quick success as a playwright and librettist in London. He also continued to work for many years as a printer, a hedge against the possibility of his failure as a dramatic writer. The first volume concentrates on the openings of his various plays. The second is a series of sketches of actors and managers with whom he worked.

Fitzgerald, Percy, 1834-1925.

159. *Memoirs of an Author* by Percy Fitzgerald. London: Richard Bentley and Son, 1895. Two Vols.

This is not so much Fitzgerald's personal recollection of his own life as an account of others whom he knew: Charles Dickens, Wilkie Collins, G.A. Sala, Edmund Yates and Charles Reade among others. Volume One includes a chapter on "Some of the Old Actors." Volume Two adds, in addition to theatrical portraits, his experiences in breaking into the theatre as a playwright and recollections of London music halls.

160. *Recollections of a Literary Man; Or Does Writing Pay?* by Percy Fitzgerald. London: Chatto and Windus, 1882. Two Vols.

Chapter Five of the first volume is devoted to Fitzgerald as a playwright: the production of his plays, rehearsals, and his friendship with Charles Mathews--a friendship which grew after Fitzgerald criticized the actor's performance in a production.

160a. *Recollections of a Literary Man* . . . A New Edition. London: Chatto and Windus, 1883. 331 pp.

Forbes-Robertson, Johnston, 1853-1937.

161. *A Player Under Three Reigns* by Sir Johnston Forbes-Robertson. London: R.G. Unwin, 1925. 291 pp.

Forbes-Robertson was distinguished as an actor, a manager, and, his first love, a portrait painter. He performed with and writes about Henry Irving, Ellen Tree and other great figures of his day. He also records the tour his own company took to Germany, Italy and America, where he met William Dean Howells and General William T. Sherman.

161a. *A Player Under Three Reigns* . . . New York: Little Brown and Co., 1925. 324 pp.

161b. *A Player Under Three Reigns* . . . Toronto: Macmillan and Co., 1925. 291 pp.

161c. *A Player Under Three Reigns.* New York: Benjamin Blom, 1971. 291 pp.

Ford, Thomas, 1829-1894.

162. *A Peep Behind the Curtain by a Boston Supernumerary.* Boston: Redding and Co., 1850. 91 pp.

Ford began his association with the theatre as a supernumerary in Boston's Tremont Theatre for twenty-five cents a night. He is candid in discussing the war between the church and the theatre, remembering vividly when the Reverend Beecher labeled the Tremont Theatre as the house of the devil on the occasion of the building's being converted to a church. Ford also gives a detailed account of the jobs and characters of individuals employed by the theatre: prompters, stage managers, carpenters, and costumers. In addition, one can go to his memoirs for an account of the actor's daily routine. He concludes with a study of the star system and its effect on the theatre's finances.

Formes, Karl Johann Franz, 1815-1899.

163. *My Memoir. Autobiography of Karl Formes.* San Francisco: J. H. Barry, Printer, 1891. 240 pp.

Formes, a German basso profundo, appeared in London with the Royal Italian Opera from 1852 to 1857 and made his first tour of America in 1857. Thereafter he divided his time between England and America. He records encounters with the outstanding singers and composers of his day (Meyerbeer, Wagner, Grisi and others) and also recounts numerous adventures, including his part in helping a "white" slave girl escape from the pre-war South.

Foster, George, 1864-

164. *Spice of Life; Sixty-Five Years in the Glamour World* by George Foster, With an Appreciation by Charles B. Cochran. Illustrated. London: Hurst and Blackett, 1939. 288 pp.

Foster, an Englishman, began his career as a singer but in the 1880s became a theatrical agent. He writes about the headliners of the 1880s and 1890s, the nature of stardom and typical salaries. He also compares conditions of the 1880s with those of the 1930s. He covers in some detail the routines of many of the old variety shows, the development of music halls, and the changing conditions under which artists and managers worked.

Foy, Eddie, 1854/56-1928.

165. *Clowning Through Life* by Eddie Foy and Alvin F. Harlow. Illustrated. New York: S.P. Dutton and Co., 1928. 331 pp.

Foy spent fifty years in show business. He gives a lively picture of theatre in the midwest and on the Great Plains in the latter part of the 19th century, telling engaging stories of his residence in Dodge City (where he earned the friendship of certain famous gunmen), his tours of cities of the Old West (Leadsville, Butte, Tombstone), and his own rise to fame. The book is filled with the names of people with whom he worked. He also describes the burning of the Iroquois Theatre in Chicago--he was on stage when the fire broke out.

Franko, Sam, 1857-1937.

166. *Chords and Discords; Memoirs and Musings of an American Musician.* New York: The Viking Press, 1938. 186 186 pp.

Franko, an American-born son of an immigrant musician, studied in Germany. After returning to the United States in 1880, he played as a violinist with the Metropolitan Concert Hall orchestra and later became its concert master. He also served for a time as concert master for Hammerstein's Manhattan Opera House. The book is arranged according to experiences in Berlin, Paris, London, Boston and New York and includes vignettes of Leopold Auer, Brahms, Victor Herbert, Hammerstein, Wagner, Offenbach and others.

Frohman, Daniel, 1851-1940.

167. *Daniel Frohman Presents; An Autobiography.* New York: C. Kendall and W. Sharp, 1935. 397 pp.

Frohman was making his own way when he was in his late teens. From a job with Horace Greeley on *The Tribune,* he moved to a position as an advance theatrical agent and then to manager of his own theatre. He, his brother Charles, and David Belasco became a threesome who controlled much of theatre in New York and contributed to the development of the combination system. His memoirs trace this development and present portraits of entertainers who dominated theatre in the last two decades of the century.

167a. *Daniel Frohman Presents . . .* New York: Lee Furman, 1937. 397 pp.

168. *Memories of a Manager; Reminiscences of the Old Lyceum and Some Players of the Last Quarter Century* by Daniel Frohman. Garden City: Doubleday, Page and Co., 1911. 235 pp.

Frohman, in writing the history of the New York Lyceum, which he organized in 1886, provides valuable insights into the constructing of a successful play, the changes that come about in any new production during rehearsals, and the separate contributions to the creation of a play made by actors, managers, and playwright. In the course of his memoir, he examines the techniques of the well-made play, including the work of Sardou, Ibsen and Barrie. Though he includes portraits of a few actors, the important focus here is on the playwright.

168a. *Memories of a Manager . . .* London: William Heinemann, 1911. 235 pp.

G

Ganthony, Robert, 1849-1931.

169. *Random Recollections* by Robert Ganthony. London: H. J. Drane, 1899. 256 pp.

Before entering show business Ganthony sampled a number of professions, including architecture, business and law. He acted, sang, played the flute, and, in preparation for a bizarre animal act, started a chicken farm. The desire to marry made him more agressive in seeking out work, so he added to his list of accomplishments, the writing of plays, ventriloquism, magic, and management.

Gardner, Major Fitzroy, 1855-

170. *Days and Ways of An Old Bohemian* by Major Fitzroy Gardner. London: John Murray, 1921. 319 pp.

Gardner's association with the English stage began in 1895 when he was invited by Beerbohm Tree to be a business manager. This led to his positions as manager for Tree, Lily Langtry and Mrs. Patrick Campbell. Garner is a good source for details about the financial side of play production.

Gatti-Casazza, Guilio, 1869-1940.

171. *Memories of the Opera* by Guilio Gatti-Casazza. New York: Scribner's Sons, 1926. 204 pp.

Gatti-Casazza, who directed in both Italy and New York, had a thorough knowledge of how opera works and how it gets on stage. For twenty-seven years he was general manager of the Metropolitan Opera in New York (beginning in 1908); previous to his Met appointment, he had directed several Italian opera companies, ranging from small "lyric theatres" to La Scala.

171a. *Memories of the Opera* . . . New York: Vienna House, 1973. 326 pp.

Gilbert, Anne Hartley, 1821-1904.

172. *Stage Reminiscences of Mrs. Gilbert.* Ed. Charlotte M. Martin. New York: Charles Scribners' Sons, 1901. 247 pp.

> Mr. and Mrs. Gilbert came to America as an acting couple shortly after their marriage in 1846. She was trained as a dancer in her youth, but perhaps because of her plain face, she was consistently cast in old women's roles. Most of her professional life was spent in the companies of Warren and Wood, Wallack, Augustin Daly and A. M. Palmer.

172a. *Stage Reminiscences of Mrs. Gilbert.* New York: Charles Scribners' Sons, 1902. 247 pp.

Glenroy, John H., 1826/28-

173. *Ins and Outs of Circus Life; Or Forty-Two Years Travel of John H. Glenroy, Bareback Rider, Through the United States, Canada, South America and Cuba.* Narrated by John E. Glenroy and Compiled by Stephen Stanley Stanford. Boston: M. M. Wing and Co., 1885. 190 pp.

> Glenroy, a circus rider, joined the circus at age seven in 1835 and worked until 1877. With various companies he toured the United States, Cuba, the West Indies, England, and South America. He records numerous anecdotes and gives a brief picture of Nashville under union occupation in 1864.

Glover, James Mackay, 1861-1931.

174. *Hims Ancient and Modern, Being the Third Book of Jimmy Glover.* New York: George H. Doran, 1926. 256 pp.

> Glover's third book of memoirs takes the form of letters of advice to a young man named Tommy who is told of Glover's first steps in the theatre, his life in opera companies, theatrical agents, elocution teachers, and "sophisticated" actresses. In the course of his instruction, he also comments on a number of non-theatrical matters such as private clubs, race problems, and South Africa.

175. *Jimmy Glover, His Book* by James M. Glover, Master of Music at Drury Lane Theatre. London: Methuen and Co., 1911. 286 pp.

> Glover writes briefly of his life in Ireland as the son of a Fenian. After he moved to London, he became involved in all kinds of musical performance: music halls, ballet, light opera and grand opera. For a

time, he also worked as a journalist. The memoirs are not only valuable for their information on the London music scene, but for pictures of nightclubs in the 1880s and 1890s and Bohemian society in London.

175a. *Jimmy Glover, His Book* . . . Third Edition. London: Methuen and Co., 1911. 299 pp.

175b. *Jimmy Glover, His Book* . . . Fourth Edition. London: Methuen and Co., 1911. 299 pp.

176. *Jimmy Glover and His Friends* by J. M. Glover. London: Chatto and Windus, 1913. 325 pp.

A second book of memoirs covering musical theatre, bohemian society, social clubs and high society.

Golden, John, 1874-1955.

177. *Stage Struck John Golden* by John Golden and Viola Brothers Shore. New York and Los Angeles: Samuel French, 1930. 321 pp.

Golden's occupations in the theatre included writing lyrics and writing and producing plays. In order to know the theatre from the inside, he got a job as a supernumerary, but soon realized that he was not an actor. Still determined to make his way in the theatre, however, he turned to songwriting and eventually created entire musical productions.

Goodale, Katherine. See Molony, Kitty.

Goodwin, Nathaniel Carl, 1857-1919.

178. *Nat Goodwin's Book* by Nat C. Goodwin. Boston: R.G. Badger, 1914. 366 pp.

Goodwin was stage-struck from his school days. With his mother's encouragement, he secured positions as supernumerary, walk-on, and understudy in Boston's professional theatres. His memoirs recount the emergence of the theatrical syndicate and the popularity of Lydia Thompson's company, a member of which he married. He also comments extensively on the efficacy of divorce.

Goodwin, Thomas, 1799-1886.

179. *Sketches and Impressions, Musical, Theatrical and Social (1799-1885) Including a Sketch of the Philharmonic Society of New York; From the After-Dinner Talk of Thomas Goodwin, Music Librarian* by R. Osgood Mason. New York and London: G. P. Putnam's Sons, 1887. 294 pp.

Goodwin, an actor, singer and musical librarian, made his first professional appearance on the stage at eight in a pantomime. In his childhood he witnessed Covent Garden's O. P. Riots, and in his young manhood he observed Mrs. Siddons and John Kemble smearing red make-up on their hands and faces for the bloody entrance in *Macbeth*. He offers sketches of theatrical personalities, Edmund Kean, George Frederick Cooke, J. B. Booth and James Wallack, and he gives a history of the Philharmonic Society and American theatre riots.

Graham, Joe F., 1850-1933.

180. *An Old Stock-Actor's Memories* With an Introduction by Dame Madge Kendal. London: Murray and Co., 1930. 305 pp.

Graham began his career performing at penny readings, moving on to become a well-known actor, manager and producer. In 1884 he became a stage manager for Frank Benson's Shakespeare company. Three bits of theatrical history are stressed in the memoirs: the career of Madge Kendal, who was his most treasured associate, the comparison of managers in 1884 with turn-of-the-century managers, and a commentary on the art of pantomime.

Grain, Richard Corney, 1884-1895.

181. *Corney Grain* by Himself. London: John Murray Co., 1888. 130 pp.

After studying for the bar, Corney Grain changed vocations and became a comic singer, making his debut in 1870 and continuing varied careers as performer, manager and writer. He comments on the many public misconception about himself: his age, his name, his marriage. He further marvels at the public's expectation that he be funny off-stage as well as on.

Gray, George, n.d.

182. *Vagaries of a Vagabond* by "the Fighting Parson" George Gray. With an Introduction by Dame Madge Kendal. London: n.p., 1930.

George Gray, who was a tramp and an itinerant as well as an actor and a parson, writes of the theatre and its interesting characters. He describes the viccisitudes of a poor actor, making his way from town to town. Unlike the typical actor turned parson, he harbors little self-righteous bitterness about this former profession.

Grimaldi, Joseph, 1778-1837.

183. *Memoirs of Joseph Grimaldi* by Charles Dickens. London: R. Bentley, 1838. Two Volumes.

As Dickens explains in his introduction, Grimaldi had been engaged in writing his memoirs for several years before his death. Dickens, only an editor, refashioned several paragraphs and did considerable cutting. Most of Grimaldi's memories are of the eighteenth century, but he continued entertaining as one of the world's foremost clowns during the first two decades of the nineteenth century, making his last appearance in public in 1828.

183a. *Memoirs . . .* New York: Stein and Day, 1838. 311 pp.

183b. *Memoirs.* Edited by "Boz" [pseud.] London, New York: G. Routledge, 1838. 258 pp.

183c. *Memoirs of Joseph Grimaldi.* Edited by "Boz" [pseud.] New York: W. H. Colyer, 1838. 232 pp.

183d. *Memoirs of Joseph Grimaldi.* Edited by "Boz." [pseud.] Philadelphia: Carey, Lea and Blanchard. 1838. Two Volumes.

183e. *Grimaldi, The Clown.* Edited by Charles Dickens. New York: H. G. Daggers, 1845. 192 pp.

183f. *Life of Joseph Grimaldi; The Noted English Clown.* Written Out From Grimaldi's Own Manuscript and Notes, Which He Left At the Time of His Death. By Charles Dickens . . . Paterson's Cheap Editions for the Millions. Philadelphia: T. B. Peterson, 184_. 192 pp.

183g. *Memoirs of Joseph Grimaldi.* Edited by "Boz.". . . London: R. Bentley, 1846. Two Volumes in One.

183h. *Joseph Grimaldi. His Life and Adventures . . .* Philadelphia: Peterson. 195_. 192 pp.

183i. *Memoirs of Joseph Grimaldi . . .* London: G. Routledge. 1853. 256 pp.

183j. *Memoirs of Joseph Grimaldi . . .* London: G. Routledge. 1854. 256 pp.

183k. *Memoirs of Joseph Grimaldi . . .* London: G. Routledge. 1866. 256 pp.

183l. *Memoirs . . .* Philadelphia: T. B. Peterson. 1866. 192 pp.

183m. *Memoirs . . .* London, New York: G. Routledge. 1869. 256 pp.

183n. *Memoirs of Joseph Grimaldi . . .* London: George Routledge. ca. 1870. 256 pp.

183o. *Memoirs . . .* London: George Routledge and Sons, 1903. 271 pp.

Grossmith, George, 1847-1912.

184. *Piano and I; Further Reminiscences* by George Grossmith. Bristol: J. W. Arrowsmith; London: Simpkin, Marshall, Hamilton, Kent and Co., 1910. 199 pp.

> This volume is a continuation of Grossmith's more lively and successful earlier memoirs. He writes entirely of his theatrical tours in the 1880s and 1890s, through Scotland, Ireland, Wales, the United States and Canada.

185. *A Society Clown. Reminiscences* by George Grossmith. Bristol: J. W. Arrowsmith; London: Simpkin, Marshall and Co., 1888. 192 pp.

> Grossmith covers his early life and career and tells how he became, in effect, a "Society Clown," a comic entertainer for high society. His first big success was with Gilbert and Sullivan, to whom he devotes considerable space. The book is anecdotal and amusing, including many letters written to him by his famous friends.

Grossmith, George, 1874-1935.

186. *"G. G."* by George Grossmith. London: Hutchinson and Co., 1933. 288 pp.

> The son, grandson and nephew of famous theatrical personalities, George Grossmith, the younger, made his debut in 1892. His family connections stood him in good stead when as a young man he secured an engagement with the Savoy Theatre of Gilbert and Sullivan. He also appeared on one occasion with the Folies Bergere, and was connected for many years with London's Gaiety Theatre.

Grossmith, Weedon, 1852-1919.

187. *From Studio to Stage: Reminiscences of Weedon Grossmith* Written by Himself. London and New York: John Lane, 1913. 367 pp.

> Weedon Grossmith was one of a number of actors who began their lives as painters. Unlike most, however, he was successful as a painter, many of his works being exhibited at the Royal Academy. Although he appeared in amateur theatricals as a young man, not until he was an established but impoverished portrait painter did he go on the stage. His first professional appearances were on tour in America, not in his native England. Toward the close of the nineteenth century he also enjoyed success as a playwright.

187a. *From Studio to Stage: Reminiscences of Weedon Grossmith.* Written by Himself. Third Ed. London: J. Lane, 1913. 367 pp.

Guilbert, Yvette, 1865-1944.

188. *Song of My Life: My Memories* by Yvette Guilbert. Trrans. Beatrice de Holthoir. London: G. G. Harrap and Co., 1929. 328 pp.

In 1883, when she was eighteen years old, Yvette Guilbert, after a girlhood of staving off poverty by doing sewing, got a small engagement at Comedy Theatre for 250 francs a month. Not until she was twenty-four did she receive a significant raise in position. One manager judged her to be all wrong for the cafe-concert performance she wished to pursue. Only in 1890 did she have any success at all. At that time she became famous as a performer at concert and cafe halls, becoming immortalized as the subject of some of the sketches of Toulouse Lautrec.

188a. *Yvette Guilbert: Struggles and Victories* by Yvette Guilbert and Harold Simpson. London: Mills and Boon, 1910.

This earlier edition of Guilbert's memoirs is included as part one of *Song of My Life*.

H

Hackett, James Henry, 1800-1871.

189. *Notes and Commentaries Upon Certain Plays and Actors of Shakespeare, With Criticisms and Correspondence* by J. H. Hackett. New York: Carleton Publishers, 1863. 353 pp.

> Hackett's commentary on Shakespare includes autobiographical material, his letters to Washington Irving, James and Horace Smith, and T. N. Talfourd, and his observations of Macready, George Vandenhoff, Edwin Forrest, the Keans, the Booths and the Kembles. His is one of those exceptional memoirs that examines acting as a craft.

189a. *Notes and Commentaries . . .* Third Ed. New York: Carleton, 1864. 353 pp.

189b. *Notes and Commentaries . . .* New York: Benjamin Blom, 1968. 353 pp.

Hare, G. Van, 1815-

190. *Fifty Years of a Showman's Life; or the Life and Travels of Van Hare* by Himself. London: W. H. Allen and Co., 1888. 418 pp.

> G. Van Hare, a master showman and circus promoter, toured the world in search of exhibitions novel to English and American audiences. He brought back cannibals, snake-charmers, and bull-fighters. His Bedouin Arab troupe was booked into some of London's largest theatres. Van Hare's memoir provides a rare look, from a showman's point of view, of nineteenth-century Africa, India, and the Far East.

190a. *Fifty Years of a Showman's Life . . .* London: Sampson, Low, Marston and Co., 1893. 418 pp.

Harker, Joseph Cunningham, 1855-1927.

191. *Studio and Stage* by Joseph C. Harker With an Introduction by Sir Johnston Forbes-Robertson. London: Nisbet and Co., 1924. 283 pp.

Harker, who found his niche in the theatre as a scene painter and designer, affords the reader a picture of the theatrical painting room, the varied theories and schools of scene design, nineteenth-century innovations in his field, and the steps taken by the scene painter in completing a design. Also included are memoirs of other famous scene designers and comments on Harker's own art by such notables as Bernard Shaw and Louis N. Parker. Harker's childhood with his widowed actress mother provides insights into the humiliation, poverty and enterprise that was often the lot of the touring actor's family.

Harman, Lindsay, 1865-

192. *A Comic Opera Life* by Lindsay Harman. West Harlepool: William Barlow, 1924. 156 pp.

After twelve years with D'Oyle Carte, Lindsay Harmon launched a twenty-year association with amateur theatrical companies, specializing in light opera. He records his memoirs of the Savoy and his problems and successes as a stage director.

Harris, Charles Kassell, 1865-1930.

193. *After the Ball; Forty Years of Melody; An Autobiography* by Charles K. Harris. New York: Frank-Maurice, 1926. 376 pp.

Harris's first success as a songwriter came when in collaboration with George Horowitz he wrote a song for Nat C. Goodwin's show, *The Skating Rink*. His versatility as a songwriter is revealed in the number of very different performers who made his show tunes famous: James J. Corbett, Al Jolson, and Adelina Patti among others. Harris prided himself on always writing his songs to fit the occasion in the show. One of his most famous hits was "After the Ball." His successes eventually allowed him in 1892 to open his own publishing house.

Hart, "Senator" Bob, 1835-1888.

194. *From Stage to Pulpit. Life of "Senator" Bob Hart, J. M. Sutherland, Twenty-Eight Years an Actor and Minstrel.* Containing One of His Burlesque Lectures. New York: C. S. Hamilton and Co., 1883. 48 pp.

Hart was variously a minstrel singer in the company of Charlie White and George Christy and a manager of Broadway and touring minstrel shows. His drinking problem led to one of the most bizarre adventures in his life--his being carried to Havanna aboard a steamer in which he had fallen asleep drunk. He gained fame by parodying scientific lectures, and includes a typical burlesque lecture on "Constitutionality of the Penal Code," heavily laced with Latin. Upon reading in a New York paper his own death after an attack of *delirium tremens*, he twice attempted suicide, eventually took the pledge and became a minister.

Hart, William Surrey, 1870-1946.

195. *My Life East and West* by William S. Hart. With Illustrations. Boston and New York: Houghton, 1929. 363 363 pp.

Before Hart became a movie cowboy he was a New York actor; he was a product of the frontier, where his father, a miller, followed his trade westward, dealing with both whites and Indians. Hart's book describes his childhood and youth on the northern plains, his occasional encounters with Indians, and his move to New York to become an actor. He played the villain Messala in the original production of *Ben Hur*. He attempted to make his many successful roles on stage and screen realistic.

195a. *My Life East and West.* New York: Benjamin Blom, 1968. 362 pp.

Harvey, John Martin, 1963-1944.

196. *The Autobiography of Sir John Martin-Harvey.* London: S. Low, Marston and Co., 1933. 563 pp.

Martin-Harvey entered the stage against the wishes of his father and, on the edge of poverty, toured the English provinces for a time. His first break was at Henry Irving's Lyceum where he came to know Gordon Craig. Like Craig, he developed an interest in sketching and painting.

196a. *The Autobiography of Sir John Martin-Harvey.* St. Clair Shores, Michigan: Scholarly Press, 1971. 563 pp.

196b. *The Autobiography of Sir John Martin-Harvey.* New York: Johnson Reprint Corp., 1971. 563 pp.

197. *The Book of Martin Harvey, With the True Story of "The Only Way" and Other Matters.* Foreward by R. B. Cunninghaeme Graham. Compiled and Edited by R.N.G.A. London: Henry Walker Publishers, 1930.

The Book of Martin Harvey contains reviews and essays written by Martin Harvey, the first of which recounts the circumstances of the writing and producing of *The Only Way*, an adaptation of *A Tale of Two Cities* created in collaboration with the Reverend Freeman Wills and the Reverend Frederick Langridge. Included are accounts of their methods of writing, the financing of the production and their creation of significant stage business.

Hauk, Minnie, 1852-1929.

198. *Memories of a Singer* by Minnie Hauk. Collated by Captain E. B. Hitchcock, Preface by A. M. Williamson. London: A. M. Philpot, 1925. 295 pp.

Minnie Hauk, an American soprano, made her operatic debut at sixteen in Brooklyn. She quickly covers incidents of her youth, including the siege of New Orleans by General Ben Butler, her debut in *La Somnabula* and her study and performances in Europe. She has chapters on her appearances in the music capitols of Europe and the famous characters with whom she was associated.

198a. *Memories of a Singer*. New York: Arno Press, 1977. 295 pp.

Hawtrey, Charles, 1858-1923.

199. *The Truth at Last From Charles Hawtrey*. Ed. W. Somerset Maugham. London: Butterworth Co., 1924. 352 pp.

Hawtrey was an English actor, playwright, and producer who was educated at Eton, Rugby, and Oxford. After breaking into theatre in London in 1889 in a production of *The Colonel*, he wrote the immensely successful play, *The Private Secretary*. He went on to become one of England's most successful producers; by the end of the century he had produced more than sixty plays. His memoirs also covers his real passion in life--horse racing.

199a. *The Truth at Last* by Charles Hawtrey. Ed. W. Somerset Maugham. Boston: Little, Brown and Co., 1924. 331 331 pp.

Hicks, Edward Seymour, 1871-1949.

200. *Between Ourselves* by Seymour Hicks. With Eight Plates. London: Cassell and Co., 1930. 252 pp.

Written twenty years after his first autobiography, this memoir characterizes the theatre of the 1880s and 1890s, recalling a "limited number of Edwardian, Georgian, and . . . Victorian celebrities" whom he knew. He recounts the murder of his father-in-law, William Terriss and the trial of Oscar Wilde, and describes judges, clubmen, bohemians, and famous wits of the period.

201. *Hail Fellow, Well Met.* London and New York: Staples Press, 1949. 206 pp.

As Hicks suggests, this memoir is a "collection of intimate glimpses of celebrities and others who . . . have become famous." Many are twentieth-century notables, but he does comment on such nineteenth-century persons as Henry Irving, Edwin Booth, Ellen Terry, George Meredith and Alfred Tennyson.

202. *Me and My Missus. Fifty Years on the Stage* by Seymour Hicks. With Twelve Half-Tone Plates. London, Toronto and Melbourne: Cassell and Co., 1939. 276 pp.

Once again, as in Hicks' other memoirs, he disregards chronological order as he writes of his early years as a professional at the Grand Theatre, Islington, and of his touring with Mr. and Mrs. Toole. Although much of this ground has already been covered in earlier memoirs, Hicks creates a different approach by devoting even more of his attention to his actress wife, Ellaline Terriss.

203. *Seymour Hicks: Twenty-Four Years of an Actor's Life.* London: Alston Rivers, 1910. 321 pp.

The first of Seymour Hicks' several autobiographical works concentrates on his early struggles to become an actor, particularly his breaking into the theatre at the Grand Theatre, Islington and his early tours of the provinces.

203a. *Seymour Hicks . . .* New York: John Lane, 1911. 321 pp.

203b. *Seymour Hicks . . .* London: C. A. Pearson, 1912. 321 pp.

Hill, Benson Earle, 1796-1845.

204. *Playing About; Or Theatrical Anecdotes and Adventures With Scenes of General Nature, From the Life; In England, Scotland, and Ireland* by Benson Earle Hill. London: The Author, Sold by W. Sams, 1840. Two Volumes.

Hill's loves were the army and the theatre. In the last profession he remained a minor player, but an associate of the best performers of his day. He writes of the Keans, the Mathews, and the Kembles. He ends his memoirs with a story of his poverty, unable to find engagements, burdened with debt, living with friends. The memoir appears to be written in part to make some money and in part to refute claims made against his character by Mrs. Mathews.

Hill, George Handel, 1809-1848.

205. *Scenes From the Life of an Actor. Compiled From the Journals, Letters, and Memoranda of the Late Yankee Hill.* With Original Illustrations, Engraved on Wood by J. W. Orr. New York: Garrett and Co., 1853. 246 pp.

Hill began his career as a supernumerary in New York, shortly afterward becoming a strolling player in halls and barns. The first ten chapters are a first-person narrative of his boyhood, his entry into show business, and the development of his "Yankee" character. The remainder of the memoirs is a mixture of third-person narrative compiled from a loose collection of Hill's memorabilia and first-person accounts of his French and English tours, his brief retirement from the stage and extraordinary matriculation as a student of medicine at Harvard University, after which he became a dental surgeon.

205a. *Scenes From the Life of an Actor.* American Culture series. 203: 8 Ann Arbor: University Microfilms, 1962. 246 pp.

205b. *Scenes From the Life of an Actor.* New York: Benjamin Blom, 1969. 246 pp.

Hodgdon, Sam K., 1853-1922.

206. *Town Hall Tonight or Show Life on the Cross Roads; The Personal Reminiscences of the Author's Ten Years' Experience as a Performer in the Small Towns of America* by Sam K. Hodgdon. Boston: 1891. 93 pp.

Hodgdon served a long apprenticeship in amateur theatricals on tour in New England, then became a minstrel performer in small touring companies. He seems never to have found engagements in urban theatres or in major touring companies. The account is notable for its minute descriptions of a poor actor's lodgings on tour: the wall plaster, the dusty floors, the wardrobes, wash stands, soap and decorations.

Holbrook, Ann Catherine, 1780-1837.

207. *Memoirs of an Actress, Comprising a Faithful Narrative of Her Theatrical Career from 1798 to the Present Period, Giving a Lively Picture of the Stage in General, And Interspersed With a Variety of Anecdotes, Humourous and Pathetic* by Ann Catherine Holbrook, Late of the New Theatre Royal, Manchester. Manchester: Printed by J. M. Harrop at the Mercury Office, 1807. 36 pp.

Although mainly concerned with the eighteenth century, this book does contain a few relevant remarks about theatre at the turn of the ninteenth century. Holbrook describes the death of her father, comedian Thomas Jackson, and comments on the difficulties facing actors in her day as well as the requirements for success. She also writes of a few actors, namely Cooke, Kemble and Master Betty.

207a. *The Dramatist; or Memoirs of the Stage* . . . An Enlarged Edition of Her "Memoir." Birmingham: Printed by Martin and Hunter, 1809. 72 pp.

Hollingshed, John, 1827-1904.

208. *Gaiety Chronicles*. Westminster: A. Constable and Co., 1898. 497 pp.

Hollingshead, an actor, director, dramatist and manager, gives a detailed account of the Gaiety Theatre under his management from its opening in 1868 until 1886. He covers all phases of theatre life: architecture, actors, plays, stage effects, and production crews. He takes credit for the first production of Ibsen in London, the first performance of the Comedie Francais in its entirety and the first matinee performances in London.

209. *"Good Old Gaiety": An Historiette and Remembrance* by John Hollingshead. London: Gaiety Theatre Co., 1903. 79 pp.

In addition to the material presented in *Gaiety Chronicles*, Hollingshead in this volume adds photographs, cast lists, play bills, and information on Gilbert and Sullivan and the Gaiety Globe Trotters.

210. *My Lifetime* by John Hollingshead, Author of Various Books (Chiefly Reprints From Magazines) and Creator of the Gaiety Theatre, With Photogravure Portrait. London: Sampson, Low, Marston and Co., 1895. Two Volumes.

Hollingshead mixes his own personal history with lengthy histories of the country and the theatre. More than most writers of theatrical memoirs, this playwright and manager places his life in the context of politics and culture external to the stage. He gives descriptions of the streets of London, its saloons, cook shops, fashions, and literary figures. At twenty-nine, after experimenting none too successfully with a number of professions, he committed himself to writinq. Later, as manager of the Gaiety, he instituted numerous reforms in the running of the company.

210a. *My Lifetime* by John Hollingshead . . . Second Edition. London: Sampson, Low, Marston and Co., 1895. Two Volumes.

Hopper, de Wolf, 1858-1935.

211. *Once a Clown, Always a Clown; Reminiscences of De Wolf Hopper* Written in Collaboration with Wesley Winans Stout. Boston: Little, Brown and Co., 1927. 238 pp.

> Like his parents, Hopper was hopelessly stage struck, even as a child. He graduated from childhood theatricals to management of his own touring company, a venture made possible with a small inheritance. Although he had one successful season as a straight actor, he soon became firmly convinced that his forte was comedy, especially the burletta, the burlesque and the musical comedy. In 1909 he left the stage for films.

211a. *Once a Clown, Always a Clown* . . . Garden City, New York: New York Publishing Co., 1927. 238 pp.

Houdin, Robert, 1805-1871.

212. *Memoirs of Robert-Houdin. Ambassador, Author, and Conjurer.* Written by Himself. London: T. W. Laurie, 1859. Two Volumes.

> Robert-Houdin was French, and only three chapters of his book pertain to England, where he appeared alternately with the Comic Opera Company and the St. James Theatre Company in 1845. A brief tour of the English provinces, Ireland and Scotland followed. He takes a look at publicity gimmicks used at the time and describes his performances before Queen Victoria and Prince Albert.

Houston, James, n.d.

213. *Autobiography of Mr. James Houston, Scottish Comedian.* Illustrated by J. M. Hamilton. Glasgow and Edinburgh: John Mengies and Co., and William Love, 1889. 196 pp.

> James Houston was a Scottish comedian who began his career in amateur dramatic clubs and concert halls. He continued to be a provincial player for the rest of his career, rarely going outside Glasgow; nevertheless, he was well enough regarded by Queen Victoria who frequented his performances. The book concludes with a selection of his songs and sketches.

Howard, J. Bannister, 1867-1946.

214. *Fifty Years a Showman* by J. Bannister Howard. With a Preface by Dame Sybil Thorndike; With Seventy-One Illustrations. London: Hutchinson and Co., 1938. 287 pp.

J. B. Howard was a theatre manager and entrepreneur for some fifty years. He was famous as the owner of theatres, cinemas, and race horses. His career in management began in the heyday of the touring system, when at one time he had fourteen shows on the road in partnership with Ben Greet. He writes about his production of such plays as *White Heather, The Great Ruby, Hearts Are Trumps, The Sign of the Cross* and *The Belle of New York*, which he calls "the most famous of all musical comedies."

Howe, J. Burdette, 1828-1908.

215. *A Cosmopolitan Actor. His Adventures All Over the World* by J. B. Howe. London: Bedford Publishing Co., 1888. 242 pp.

In his capacity as actor and manager, Howe travelled many times between England and America, touring both countries extensively. In addition to his theatrical portraits, he gives his impressions of immigrant passage to America in what he describes as the Black Hole of Calcutta. He writes of the American Civil War and of New York City jails, which he saw as an inmate. India, Hawaii and Australia are a few of the countries he describes.

Hubbard, Elbert, 1856-

216. *In the Spotlight. Personal Experiences of Elbert Hubbard on The American Stage.* East Aurora, New York: The Roycrofters, 1917. 134 pp.

Hubbard, a dramatist, entertainer and essayist, relates his experiences in vaudeville at the Majestic Theatre, Chicago, and on the Orpheum Circuit. He also comments on actors and acting and on the conflict between church and stage.

Hurst, Lulu, n.d.

217. *Lulu Hurst (The Georgia Wonder,) Writes Her Autobiography and For the First Time Explains and Demonstrates The Great Secret of Her Marvelous Power.* Rome, Georgia: The Lulu Hurst Book Co., 1897. 267 pp.

Lulu Hurst, a fourteen-year-old girl billed as a psychic witch with the "Power," could with the touch of a hand toss strong men and women around the stage. After an extensive tour of South Carolina and Georgia, she took Washington, New York and the far west by storm. Charles Frohman managed her appearances at Wallacks when Lily Langtry, an eager volunteer for Hurst's act, ended up rumpled, bruised and humiliated. Hurst's amazing relation at book's end is that her "power" was, from the beginning, a series of tricks based on her personal discovery of certain physical laws. She describes and graphically illustrates each trick in detail.

Hutchison, Percy, 1875-1945.

218. *Masquerade* by Percy Hutchison. London: G. G. Harrap and Co., 1936. 286 pp.

Much of Hutchison's memoir is about his uncle, Charles Wyndham, who encouraged him and managed his early career on stage. He includes a portrait of Edward, Prince of Wales, and gives an estimate of the monarch's influence on the theatre. Edward's support, writes Hutchison, elevated the theatre to a respectable position which it had never before enjoyed in England.

J

Janis, Elsie, 1889-1956.

219. *So Far So Good! An Autobiography* by Elsie Janis. New York: E.P. Dutton and Co., 1932. 344 pp.

> Elsie Janis made her debut at the age of five in the year 1894 in a local Columbus, Ohio, stock company. Her mother, eager to advance her daughter's career, secured her a second engagement with a Buffalo vaudeville company. At eight she made her New York debut. Janis gives an account of the Gerry Society, which looked after the interests of child performers in New York; children could be hired as actors, she reports, but not as singers or dancers.

219a. *So Far So Good! An Autobiography* . . . London: J. Long, 1933. 287 pp.

Jefferson, Joseph, 1829-1905.

220. *The Autobiography of Joseph Jefferson*. New York: The Century Co., 1890. 501 pp.

> Like many personal memoirs of actors, Jefferson's famous work is a history of the American theatre. He describes the primitive conditions under which his father and mother performed when he was a child, the development of his most famous roles, and his association with legendary characters like Laura Keene and Mrs. John Drew. He continually offers a defense of his profession at the same time that he insists on the highest standards of performance from its members.

220a. *The Autobiography of Joseph Jefferson*. London: T. Fisher Unwin Co., 1890. 501 pp.

220b. *The Autobiography of Joseph Jefferson*. New York: The Century Co., 1897. 509 pp.

220c. *The Autobiography of Joseph Jefferson.* New York: The Century Co., 1917. 509 pp.

220d. *"Rip Van Winkle"; The Autobiography of Joseph Jefferson.* London: Reinhardt and Evans, 1949. 375 pp.

220e. *"Rip Van Winkle"* . . . New York: Appleton-Century Crofts, 1950. 375 pp.

220f. *The Autobiography of Joseph Jefferson.* Ed. Alan S. Downer. Cambridge, Mass.: The Belnap Press of Harvard University Press, 1964. 363 pp.

Jerome, Jerome K., 1859-1927.

221. *On the Stage - And Off; The Brief Career of A Would-Be Actor* by Jerome K. Jerome. New York: Minerva Publishing Co., 188-. 201 pp.

> Jerome K. Jerome discusses in some detail, but in no particular order, stage make-up, elocution, theatre agents, the securing of parts, and backstage activity. He describes the paint room, the wardrobe room, the behavior of "supers" on and off stage and the headaches of finding lodgings while on tour. He includes a dramatic recreation of what he saw as a typical rehearsal in a minor touring company. Jerome's theatrical career was brief, third-rate, and, as he so skillfully describes it, hilarious.

221a. *On the Stage* . . . London: Leadenhall Press, 1885. 219 pp.

221b. *On the Stage* . . . London: Leadenhall Press, 1891. 219 pp.

221c. *On the Stage* . . . Fifteenth Edition. London: Leadenhall Press, Simpkin, Marshall, n. d. 219 pp.

221d. *On the Stage* . . . New York: Charles Scribner's Sons, 1891. 170 pp.

221e. *On the Stage* . . . New York: Holt and Co., 1891. 170 pp.

221f. *On the Stage* . . . Boston: Raymond Co., 1891. 262 pp.

221g. *On the Stage* . . . Leadenhall Press, 1908. 160 pp.

Jupp, James, n. d.

222. *Gaiety Stage Door; Thirty Years of Reminiscences of the Theatre* by James Jupp. With an Introduction by Mabel Russell Philipson. M.P., London: J. Cape, 1923. 352 pp.

James Jupp, not an actor nor a manager but a stage door keeper, presents the reader with interesting material from an unusual perspective. Here one can find details of George Edwardes' rehearsals, his use of puppets in a scale model of the set, and his blocking of the chorus. Jupp has anecdotes about the successes and the failures--all the stage struck people who had no chance to succeed: the wealthy matrons, the failed priests, and the talentless youths. He also offers an eye-witness account of the murder of William Terriss.

K

Kean, Charles John, 1811-1868, and Tree, Ellen, 1805-1880.

223. *Emigrant in Motley: The Journey of Charles and Ellen Kean in Quest of a Theatrical Fortune in Australia and America as Told in Their Hitherto Unpublished Letters.* Ed. J. M. D. Hardwick With a Foreword by Anthony Quayle. London: Rockliff Co., 1954. 260 pp.

> This collection of letters covers thiry years, from 1830 to 1860. Most of them record years spent in America and include arrangements made for appearances, salaries, and estimates of fellow actors. In addition, the couple reveals their impressions of the south, slavery, secession, the civil war and Abraham Lincoln.

224. *Letters of Mr. and Mrs. Charles Kean, Relating to Their American Tours.* Ed. Wiliam Glasgow Bruce Carson. Washington University Studies. New Series. Language and Literature No. 15. St. Louis: Washington University Press, 1945. 181 pp.

> In correspondence of the Keans to friends and relatives, written in the last years of colonial touring, 1862-1866, they describe managers, supporting players, ocean voyages, hotel accommodations, and the properties and costumes that were so important to their spectacular productions. Ellen's letters are preoccupied with the weather and her own and other people's ailments. Charles' letters are mainly about business negotiations.

Keeler, Ralph, 1840-1873.

225. *Vagabond Adventures.* Cambridge: Welch, Bigelow and Co., n. d. 274 pp.

> Ralph Keeler was an orphan who took to the stage as a minstrel performer when he was in his early teens. He worked in the companies of Ford and Kunkel and Johnny

Booker. His first jobs were dancing and preparing an acid-flavored drink that was sold as lemonade. His last engagement was aboard the Floating Palace where he came to know the boxers, gamblers, acrobats and musicians attached to river entertainments.

225a. *Vagabond Adventures*. Boston: Fields, Osgood and Co., 1870. 274 pp.

225b. *Vagabond Adventures*. Boston: J. R. Osgood and Co., 1872. 274 pp.

225c. *Vagabond Adventures*. Boston: n. p., 1876.

Kellar, Harry, 1849-1922.

226. *A Magician's Tour Up and Down and Round About the Earth, Being the Life and Adventures of the American Nostradamus; Harry Kellar*. Edited by His Faithful "Familiar,""Satan Junior." Chicago: R.R. Donnelley and Sons, 1886. 214 pp.

Kellar established a career for himself as a spiritualist in his youth and took his show on world tours. Mexico, Cuba, India, Africa and Australia are all described in his account. In 1885, back in the United States, he played for 179 consecutive performances at the Comedy Theatre on Broadway.

Kellogg, Charles, n. d.

227. *Charles Kellogg. The Nature Singer. His Book*. Morgan Hill, California: Pacific Science Press, 1929. 243 243 pp.

Kellogg, who was reared in the wilderness of the California frontier among Indians, prospectors and Chinese workers, spent twenty years on the lecture platform and fifteen years on the stage. The book he writes covers vignettes of people and customs of the frontier, vaudeville, the Fiji Islands and Paris, places which he toured with his woodsman act.

Kellogg, Clara, 1842-1916.

228. *Memoirs of an American Prima Donna* by Clara Louise Kellogg (Mme Strakosch) With Forty Illustrations. New York and London: G.P. Putnam's Sons, 1913. 382 pp.

Clara Kellogg first sang in public in New York City in 1861 at the age of nineteen and for twenty-five years she was one of the foremost singers in America. She retired from the stage in 1887 at the time of her marriage to her manager. She writes of her extensive voice and music training and of a number of celebrated musicians with whom she worked. She was friendly with artists in other fields and presents character studies of Longfellow and Oliver Wendell Holmes. Of particular interest is her estimate of the great influence of black music and minstrels on her own classical mode.

228a. *Memoirs of an American Prima Donna.* New York: Da Capo Press, 1978. 382 pp.

Kelly, Michael, 1764-1826.

229. *Reminiscences of Michael Kelly of the Kings Theatre and Theatre Royal, Drury Lane, Including a Period of Nearly Half a Century; With Anecdotes of Many Distinguished Persons.* New York: Printed by J. and J. Harper for Collins and Hannay, 1826. Two Vols.

Kelly, a brilliant tenor and a mediocre composer, covers his life from musical studies at age seven in 1771 until 1826. After studying voice in Naples, where he appeared in Italian opera under the name of Occhelli, and later singing in Vienna, where he came to know Mozart well, he moved to London in 1787 and sang there until his retirement, appearing primarily at Drury Lane. His account of Mozart is reputedly one of the best in English. He also describes Haydn, Gluck, Mrs. Siddons, Kean, the Kembles and many others.

229a. *Reminiscences of Michael Kelly . . .* Second Edition. London: H. Colburn, 1826. Two Vols.

229b. *Reminiscences of Michael Kelly . . .* Another Issue. New York: Printed by J. and J. Harper for E. Duyckinck, Collins, and Hannay, 1826. Two Vols.

229c. *Reminiscences of Michael Kelly . . .* New York: Da Capo Press, 1968. Two Vols.

229d. *Reminiscences of Michael Kelly . . .* New York: Benjamin Blom, 1969. 424 pp.

229e. *Solo Recital; The Reminiscences of Michael Kelly . . .* Abridged Edition. London: Folio Society, 1972. 372 pp.

229f. *Reminiscences of Michael Kelly . . .* London and New York: Oxford University Press, 1975. 369 pp.

Kelly, Walter C., 1873-1939.

230. *Of Me I Sing, An Informal Autobiography.* New York: Dial Press, 1953. 246 pp.

Kelly spent four years in the United States Navy as a machinist during the Spanish-American War and worked in the shipyards of Newport News, Virginia, before becoming a performer. He describes something of the background of the period: the boarding houses, the tent cities in the booming times of Newport News, the atmosphere of the saloons, and the elections of 1896. In particular, he tells of the trail of several Negroes at the local courthouse with Judge John Dudley Brown presiding. It was this that provided the inspiration for his later monologues as "The Virginia Judge."

Kemble, Frances Anne, 1809-1893.

231. *Further Records, 1848-1883: A Series of Letters, Forming a Sequel to Records of a Girlhood, and Records of Later Life.* London: R. Bentley and Sons, 1890. Two Vols.

Fanny Kemble had virtually retired from stage appearances and readings by the time these memoirs-- largely letters to which she adds transition-- begin. However, much of her subject matter is still her earlier profession, particularly her distaste for the stage and the moral conflict she felt between her need for reality and her life of illusion on the stage. These later memoirs contain her impressions of famous men and women of her time: Henry Ward Beecher, Margaret Fuller, Garibaldi, Bret Hart and Longfellow.

231a. *Further Records* . . . New York: H. Holt and Co., 1891. 380 pp.

231b. *Further Records* . . . New York: Benjamin Blom, 1972. Two Vols. in One.

232. *Journal* by Frances Anne Butler. London: J. Murray, 1835. Two Vols.

Fanny Kemble's journal covers the 1832-1833 theatrical season from her departure from England for her American tour with her father until just before her marriage to Pierce Butler and her farewell to the stage. Here she comments on American manners and society, the American clergy's view of the stage and attitudes of American women.

232a. *Journal* . . . Philadelphia: Carey, Lea and Blanchard, 1835. Two Vols.

232b. *Journal* . . . American Culture Series 103:2. Ann Arbor: University Microfilms, 1960. Two Vols.

232c. *Journal* . . . New York: Benjamin Blom, 1970. Two Vols. in One.

232d. *Journal of a Residence in America* by Fanny Anne Butler (Miss Fanny Kemble) Brussels: A. Wahlen, 1835. 326 pp.

232e. *Journal of a Residence in America* . . . New York: Harper and Brothers, 1863. 337 pp.

233. *Journal of a Residence on a Georgia Plantation . . .* London: Longman, Green, Longman, Roberts and Green, 1863. 434 pp.

Fanny Kemble's journal covers the years 1838-1839 during her residence in Georgia. The record has nothing to do with the theatre, but she brings to the subject of slavery an independence of mind and strength of character, encouraged in large part by her past theatrical associations. She writes of conditions as she found them and of her own constantly thwarted attempts to educate, rescue and heal those who learned to appeal to her for relief.

233a. *Journal of a Residence . . .* New York: Harper and Brothers, 1864. 337 pp.

233b. *Journal of a Residence . . .* American Culture Series 167: 3 Ann Arbor: University Microfilms, 1961. 337 pp.

233c. *Journal of a Residence . . .* New York: Knopf, 1961. 415 pp.

233d. *Journal of a Residence . . .* Chicago: Afro-American Press, 1969. 337 pp.

234. *Record of a Girlhood* by Frances Anne Kemble. London: Richard Bentley and Son, 1878. Three Vols.

Fanny Kemble's record of her girlhood begins with a history of her theatrical family, her idyllic girlhood and French education. Of particular interest in this volume is the way in which her career on the stage began, much against her will, as a means of retrieving the family's fortune, and her phenomenal success in England and America. The account ends with her marriage to Pierce Butler.

234a. *Record of a Girlhood . . .* Second Edition. London: Richard Bentley and Son, 1879. Three Vols.

234b. *Record of a Girlhood . . .* Third Edition. London: Richard Bentley and Son, 1879. Three Vols.

234c. *Record of a Girlhood . . .* New York: H. Holt and Co., 1879. 605 pp.

234d. *Record of a Girlhood . . .* Second Edition. New York: H. Holt and Co., 1883. 605 pp.

234e. *Record of a Girlhood . . .* New York: H. Holt and Co., 1884. 605 pp.

235. *Records of Later Life* by Frances Anne Kemble. London: Richard Bentley and Son, 1882. Three Vols.

These volumes consist of memoirs, parts of journals, and letters to which Fanny Kemble has added transitional explanations. They cover a period from her marriage to Pierce Butler to her return to the stage in England. She gives an account of the shocking revelations she had concerning her husband's Quaker family and their strait-laced society, her first encounter with primitive southern living conditions, her observations of slavery, and the growth of her theories of motherhood and women's rights. The last half describes the family's stay in Europe, the dissolution of her marriage after the return to Philadelphia, and her return to the stage after Pierce Butler forced her to leave his house and their children.

235a. *Records of Later Life . . .* New York: H. Holt and Co., 1882. 676 pp.

235b. *Records of Later Life . . .* New York: H. Holt and Co., 1884. 676 pp.

236. *A Year of Consolation* by Mrs. Butler, Late Fanny Kemble. London: E. Moxon, 1847. Two Vols.

This is a book of her travels in France and Italy in 1845 and has no reference to the theatre.

236a. *A Year of Consolation . . .* New York: Wiley and Putnam, 1847. Two Vols. in One.

236b. *A Year of Consolation . . .* New York: J. Wiley, 1849. Two Vols. in One.

236c. *A Year of Consolation . . .* Hartford: S. Andrus and Co., 1851. Two Vols. in One.

Kendal, Madge, 1849-1935.

237. *Dame Madge Kendal; By Herself.* Editor's Note by Rudolph de Cordova. London: J. Murray, 1933. 313 pp.

Dame Kendal writes of her courtship and marriage, her decision to always be leading lady to her husband, and their tragic problems with their children. She ends her story with an account of her charities, most notably her famous friendship with John Merrick, "The Elephant Man."

238. *Dramatic Opinions* by Mrs. Kendal. Boston: Little, Brown and Co., 1890. 180 pp.

Mrs. Kendal gives an account of her family, her stage appearances as a child, her education and marriage. She giver her "opinions" of amateurs, drama critics, training for the stage, playwrights and acting couples.

238a. *Dramatic Opinions . . .* Woodchester, Gloucester: Arthur Press, 1925. 61 pp.

Kerr, Frederick, 1858-1933.

239. *Recollections of a Defective Memory* by Fred Kerr. London: T. Butterworth, 1930. 285 pp.

Kerr, the son of an English solicitor, was educated at Cambridge and broke into theatre in New York after working for a time as a caricaturist. He played supporting roles with Madame Selina Delora and Lester Wallack's companies, and, after several tours, achieved relatively stable success with Pinero in *The Magistrate*. He gives vignettes of a great many performers with whom he worked, and comments on critics, actors, audiences, golf, cricket, English and American clubs, and the murder of William Terriss.

Kingston, Gertrude, 1866/69-1937.

240. *Curtsy While You're Thinking* by Gertrude Kingston. London: Williams and Norgate, 1937. 307 pp.

Childhood and family connections play a fairly significant part in this autobiographical story. Kingston (Mrs. George Silver), was an actress, manager, and producer, born into a family with prestigious theatre connections. Her family knew Richard and Cosima Wagner, Henry Irving, Oscar Wilde, Frank Miles and Sarah Bernhardt. Kingston describes her study of painting in Berlin and Paris and her study of theatre under Sarah Thorne.

Knowles, Richard George, 1858-1919.

241. *A Modern Columbus* by R. G. Knowles. His Voyages, His Travels, His Discoveries . . . London: T. W. Laurie, n. d. 301 pp.

Knowles, a Canadian by birth, made his career as an actor in the United States. He worked briefly in New York with the elder Cohan, Charles Hoyt and B. F. Keith in vaudeville, minstrel and variety companies. He writes about his experiences with Haverly's, Daly's, and the London music halls and about his tours of Australia, New Zealand, South Africa, India, and China.

241a. *A Modern Columbus . . .* London: T. W. Laurie, 1915. 301 pp.

L

Laceby, Arthur, 1879-1967.

243. *Footlights and Fistfights, and Femmes; the Jimmy Lake Story* As Told to Helen Giblo. First Edition. New York: Vantage Press, 1957. 252 pp.

> Lake describes himself as a burlesque comedian, fight official, and manager of shows, hotels, and nightclubs. As a child he worked around the saloons, flophousesand whore houses in the Chinatown opium dens of New York City in the 1880s and 1890s. His first introductions to show business were in seedy music halls, Barnum's museum and other museums where stock companies played. Before he was twenty he and his partner, Mahoney, played with Lillian Russell, De Wolf Hopper, and Tony Pastor. New York City in the 1880s and '90s and the living conditions of the small-time vaudeville performer are graphically described.

Lang, Matheson, 1879-1948.

244. *Mr. Wu Looks Back; Thoughts and Memories* by Matheson Lang. With Twenty-Four Half-Tone Illustrations. London: S. Paul and Co., 1941. 224 pp.

> Lang, who began his career with Louis Calvert's company on tour, later became assistant stage manager for a touring melodrama. Subsequently he worked as an actor and a manager, touring the West Indies, South Africa and the Far East. Major parts of the book deal with Lily Langtry, the Lyceum Theatre, his management of a tour of South Africa, the character of "Mr. Wu," his most famous creation, and productions of Shakespeare at the Old Vic.

Langtry, Lily, 1852-1929.

245. *The Days I Knew* by Lily Langtry (Lady de Bathe) With a Foreword by Richard le Gallienne. With Seventy-Seven Illustrations. London: Hutchinson and Co., 1925. 319 pp.

Lily Langtry made her stage debut when she was already famous as a beauty and a member of prominent social circles in England. The reader learns more about society and the people Lily knew than about the theatre of the period. She covers her girlhood in Jersey, and her first marriage, her stage career in England, and her tours to America and South Africa. She makes a good story of her visit to "Judge" Roy Bean's town of Langtry, Texas, named for her.

245a. *The Days I Knew . . .* New York: George H. Doran Co., 1925. 300 pp.

Lano, David, 1874-

246. *A Wandering Showman I.* East Lansing: Michigan State University Press, 1957. 290 pp.

A puppeteer and son of generations of traveling entertainers, Lano ran away from home at fourteen with only a legacy of puppets and puppet-making learned from his grandfather. Before he set out on his own, he traveled with his parents and grandparents throughout Virginia, Kentucky and Tennessee, often making less than three dollars a performance. As a member of a circus troupe, his associates were knife-throwners, fire-eaters and snake charmers.

Lauder, Harry, 1870-1950.

247. *Between You and Me* by Sir Harry Lauder. Toronto: McClelland and Stewart, 1919. 324 pp.

The first five chapters of Harry Lauder's book are about his childhood and begining appearances as singer, comic, and amateur contest performer. The remainder is devoted to his successful career in the twentieth century, as is his *Harry Lauder at Home and on Tour.*

247a. *Between You and Me . . .* New York: The James McCann Co., 1919. 324 pp.

248. *Roamin' in the Gloamin'* by Sir Harry Lauder. London: Hutchinson and Co., 1928. 287 pp.

After a poverty-stricken childhood working at such hard occupations as wagoning and coal mining, Harry Lauder began to play music in a Scottish temperance band and work on his singing and comic routines for amateur performances. He went on to engagements at Glasgow music halls and professional tours. The tours forced him, reluctantly, to give up coal mining entirely. His real professional break did not come until the twentieth century.

248a. *Roamin' in the Gloamin'* . . . New York: Grosset and Dunlap, 1928. 300 pp.

Lazarovich-Hrebelianovich. See Calhoun, Eleanor.

Leathes, Edmund, 1847-1891.

249. *An Actor Abroad, or Gossip Dramatic, Narrative and Descriptive From the Recollections of an Actor in Australia, New Zealand, the Sandwich Islands, California, Nevada, Central America, and New York*. London: Hurst and Blackett, 1880. 317 pp.

> Leathes' book is a travel book as well as a theatrical memoir. As a supporting actor, he appeared in theatres in Australia, New Zealand, Hawaii and in all parts of the United States. He describes not only the areas through which he travels, but those details that make the theatres in each place unique to the area.

Leavitt, Michael Bennett, 1843-1935.

250. *Fifty Years in Theatrical Management* by M. B. Leavitt; With Reproductions of Over Five Hundred Photographs. New York: Broadway Publishing Co., 1912. 735 pp.

> Leavitt recounts his fifty years as a manager and theatre promoter--a career which began as a minstrel player. His retirement from show business was set aside with the financial panic of 1893, which may also have prompted him to begin work on his memoirs. Leavitt's book is very valuable for its information about areas of show business beyond legitimate theatre: varieties, vaudeville, minstrels, circuses, dime museums, sea resort entertainments, wild west shows, pantomimists, bands and nickelodeons.

Lee, Henry, 1765-1836.

251. *Memoirs of a Manager, or Life's Stage With New Scenery* Briefly Sketched by Henry Lee. Taunton: Printed by W. Bragg, by Simpkin and Marshall, 1830. Two Vols. in One.

> Lee was a dramatist, actor, and manager. Leaving home at twenty-four to become an actor, he toured the provinces and the Channel Islands, later became a manager and dramatist. The memoirs are written in no particular order, and, somewhat oddly, he tells nothing about his career as a manager. In the two volumes, biographical reminiscences are interspersed with letters written to him, poems, random anecdotes, and defenses of the stage.

Lehmann, Lilli, 1848-1929.

252. *My Path Through Life* by Lilli Lehmann. Translated

by Benedict Seligman. New York and London: G. P. Putnam's Sons, 1914. 510 pp.

Lehman, a coloratura soprano from Germany, made her operatic debut in Prague in 1865. She writes of her tours of Europe as well as her many years in America and includes a list of her 117 roles. She was married to Paul Kalish, a singer from New York.

252a. *My Path Through Life . . .* New York: E. P. Dutton, 1918. 232 pp.

252b. *My Path Through Life . . .* New York: E. P. Dutton, 1920. 232 pp.

252c. *My Path Through Life . . .* New York: Arno Press, 1977. 510 pp.

252d. *My Path Through Life . . .* New York: Da Capo Press, 1980. 232 pp.

Lehmann, Liza, 1862-1918.

253. *The Life of Liza Lehmann* by Herself. London: T. Fisher Unwin, 1918. 232 pp.

Lehmann, a concert singer, recalls her musical career as a performer and composer. She describes the process of composing certain works, her meetings with musical and literary figures, and she includes press reviews.

253a. *The Life of Liza Lehmann.* New York: E. P. Dutton, 1919. 232 pp.

253b. *The Life of Liza Lehmann.* New York: Dutton and Co., 1920. 232 pp.

253c. *The Life of Liza Lehmann.* New York: Da Capo Press, 1980. 232 pp.

Leman, Walter Moore, 1810-

254. *Memories of an Old Actor* by Walter M. Leman. San Francisco: A. Roman Co., 1886. 406 pp.

After many years as a stock actor in the Booth Theatres, Walter Leman sought his fortune in California, the mining camps of the far west, and Honolulu. The first half of his memoir is a series of estimates of great actors whom he saw or performed with in the east. The second half, about the American frontier, comes alive with details about the everyday life of the strolling player in the far west.

254a. *Memories of an Old Actor.* St. Clair Shores, Michigan: Scholarly Press, 1969, 406 pp.

Lena, Dan, 1860-1904.

255. *Dan Leno - Hys Book* Written by Himself. Edited by John Duncan With an Introduction by Roy Hudd. London: H. Evelyn, 1968. 60 pp.

This is a whimsical fragment in which Leno, whose real name is George Galvin, tells of his introduction to the stage as a child, his clog dancing, a misadventure he had during a performance in Liverpool, and a command performance at Windsor Castle.

Leverton, William Henry, 1866-1941.

256. *Through the Box-Office Window; Memories of Fifty Years at the Haymarket Theatre* by W. H. Leverton ("Bill") in Collaboration with J. B. Booth: With a Foreword by Marie Tempest. With 31 Illustrations. London: T. W. Laurie, 1932. 245 pp.

William Henry Leverton, for fifty years box office keeper of one of London's most famous theatres--the Haymarket--recounts numerous anecdotes of managers and actors of his acquaintance. There is very little information here about the operation of theatres.

Lindsay, Hugh, 1804-

257. *History of the Life, Travels and Incidents of Col. Hugh Lindsay, the Celebrated Comedian For a Period of Thirty-Seven Years.* Written by Himself. Philadelphia: no publisher given, 1859. 96 pp.

As a child, Hugh Lindsay was indentured by his parents to a cruel master. He escaped and began his life in show business as a circus clown in rural Pennsylvania. In addition to his many other duties, he drove the circus elephants and camels from town to town, living close to danger among gamblers, drunks and thieves. For years he lived from his proceeds as a part owner of a circus and a tavern. However, at the time of his book's appearance, his imbibing of a poisonous, nearly fatal, drink of whiskey had led to his conversion and a new career as a temperance lecturer.

257a. *History of the Life, Travels and Incidents . . .* Macungie, Pennsylvania: O. P. Knauss, 1883. 60 pp.

Livingstone, Belle, 1875-

258. *Belle of Bohemia - The Memoirs of Belle Livingstone.* London: John Hamilton, 1927. 318 pp.

This is the first of two volumes of memoirs which cover the same years in Belle Livingstone's life--her childhood on the frontier, her first job in a chorus in

Chicago, touring, her introduction to New York theatre in the 1890s and her entrance into London and Paris society after a surprise legacy. She gives particular attention to the "fast" social life of the Prince of Wales.

259. *Belle Out of Order.* New York: Henry Holt and Co., 1959. 341 pp.

The second volume of Belle Livingstone' memoirs covers much of the same ground of the earlier book: her job as a chorus girl for forty-five dollars a week, her tours in the 1890s, the life spent in cheap restaurants and crowded trains and her opening in New York. Some information can be found here on celebrities she knew: Charles Dana Gibson, P. T. Barnum, Lord Kitchener and the Prince of Wales.

Lloyd, James, 1846-1909.

260. *My Circus Life. Being the Life and Adventures and the World Travels and Experiences of an Artist and Circus Proprietor Now Aged Seventy-Nine Years. The Last of the Mohicans Emanated From "The Cradle of the Circus World," Astley's Amphitheatre, Westminster Bridge Road, London.* London: Noel Douglas, 1925. 102 pp.

Lloyd's father was employed by Astley's for thirty years and saw his son "Jimmy" become a dancer and horseback rider as a child. Because Lloyd was not allowed in school as a young man, he taught himself to read by learning the names written over shops. These memoirs, written in very short, simple, child-like sentences, picture a melancholy life interrupted by numerous show business accidents and unhappily burdened by marriage and children.

Logan, Olive, 1839/41-1909.

261. *Before the Footlights and Behind the Scenes. A Book About "the Show Business" in All Its Branches: From Puppet Shows to Grand Opera; From Mountebanks to Menageries; From Learned Pigs to Lectures; From Burlesque Blondes to Actors and Actresses . . .* by Olive Logan. Philadelphia: Parmelee and Co.; San Francisco: H. H. Bancroft and Co., 1870. 612 pp.

Olive Logan, the daughter of travelling actors, was for many years a reluctant actress and an enthusiastic author. Her memoirs comprise one of the most comprehensive accounts of theatre operation in the nineteenth century. Although Logan is decidedly opinionated, she offers objective details about backstage employment, rehearsals, circus life and the families of show people--details that are found in few other places.

262. *The Mimic World, and Public Exhibitions; Their History, Their Morals and Effects.* Philadelphia: New World Publishing Co., 1871. 590 pp.

Logan's second memoir is much like the first. In this one, however, she eliminates two of her chapters in which she had asked the reader to put aside prejudices about the theatre. Unlike the first memoir, the second one, because of these and other changes, has a more decided tone of Puritanical condemnation of what she judged to be immoral among stage folk.

Ludlow, Noah Miller, 1795-1866.

263. *Dramatic Life As I Found It. A Record of Personal Experience in the West and South, With Anecdotes and Biographical Sketches of the Principal Actors and Actresses Who Have at Times Appeared Upon the Stage in the Mississippi Valley* by N. M. Ludlow. St. Louis: G. I. Jones and Co., 1880. 733 pp.

Noah Ludlow was involved in most of the major pioneer theatrical developments of the nineteenth century. His career began in the towns of the northeast, where he joined Samuel Drake in his tour down to Kentucky and Tennessee. As a manager and actor, Ludlow helped establish theatre in the Mississippi Valley. Like his partner Sol Smith, Ludlow is at his best in describing performances in small towns along his circuit. He also includes biographical sketches of virtually every major English and American actor who toured the United States.

263a. *Dramatic Life As I Found It . . .* Introduction by Francis Hodge. New York: Benjamin Blom 1966. 779 pp.

Lumley, Benjamin, 1811-1875.

264. *Reminiscences of the Opera* by Benjamin Lumley, Twenty Years Director of Her Majesty's Theatre. London: Hurst and Blackett, 1864. 448 pp.

Lumley was for twenty years director of Her Majesty's Theatre. His strictly professional autobiography includes nothing of the private lives of himself or others. Instead, his is a story of how a manager or director keeps an expensive artistic venture alive without sacrificing quality, balance or freshness. It was a matter of great pride with Lumley that he introduced many Italian and German operas into England.

Luttrell, Gladys. See Anon. *Letters of an Actress.*

Lynn, H. S.

265. *The Adventures of a Strange Man.* Dr. H. S. Lynn.

With a Supplement Showing "How It's Done." No Publisher, 1873. 88 pp.

Lynn's childhood prediliction for magic and the education in magic he received from the many foreign countries he visited as a sailor, led to his career as a performer. He includes advertisements, programs which describe each trick of the performance in detail, and descriptions of Virginia City, of mining camps and of Mormonism.

Lytton, Henry Alfred, 1860/65/67-1936.

266. *The Secrets of A Savoyard* by Henry A. Lytton. London: Jarrolds, 1922. 191 pp.

As a musical comedy star, Lytton was identified closely with Gilbert and Sullivan productions at the Savoy Theatre. His memoirs contain descriptions of music halls, burlesque and light opera, studies of Gilbert and Sulllivan and their break-up, and comments on Edward, Prince of Wales. He concludes with stories of twelve operettas.

266a. *The Secrets of a Savoyard.* London: Jarrolds, 1927. 191 pp.

267. *A Wandering Minstrel, Reminiscences* by Sir Henry Lytton. Second Impression. London: Jarrold, 1933. 287 pp.

Henry Lytton's second memoir is about his youth, his first years in the D'Oyly Carte Company, and his tours of China and America in the twentieth century.

267a. *A Wandering Minstrel . . .* Third Impression. London: Jarrolds, 1933. 287 pp.

M

MacCarthy, Lillah, 1857-1960.

268. *Myself and My Friends* by Lillah MacCarthy, O.B.E. (Lady Keeble) With an Aside by Bernard Shaw. London: T. Butterworth, 1933. 319 pp.

> Lillah MacCarthy made her first amateur stage appearance at age fifteen in 1890 as Lady Macbeth. On the strength of advice from Frank Benson that she be trained, her father sold their house and moved the whole family to London so that she could attend Hermann Vezin's School of Acting. She secured London engagements, was praised by Shaw, toured the provinces with Ben Greet, and returned to the Lyric Theatre with a contract with Wilson Barrett that would last for eight years and include tours of Australia and South Africa.

268a. *Myself and My Friends . . .* New York: Dutton, 1933. 319 pp.

Mackintosh, Matthew, n.d.

269. *Stage Reminiscences: Being Recollections Chiefly Personal, of Celebrated Theatrical and Musical Performers During the Last Forty Years By An Old Stager.* Glasgow: James Hedderwick and Son, 1866. 236 pp.

> Mackintosh was a backstage machinist, carpenter, man-Friday, drinking companion, baby-sitter, errand runner, and on-stage assistant in equestrian acts. He also worked as advance agent, horse-caretaker and property man. The job of which he writes most proudly, however, is one which required him to refashion stages and install gas lights.

269a. *Stage Reminiscences . . .* Second edition. Glasgow: James Hedderwick and Son, 1870. 236 pp.

Macready, William charles, 1793-1874.

270. *Diaries of William Charles Macready 1833-1851.* Ed. William Toynbee. With Forty-Nine Portraits. London: Chapman and Hall, 1912. Two Vols.

As Toynbee noted in the introduction, Macready began these diaries in 1833, at the height of his reputation. They reveal the daily routine of an actor, sometimes hour-by-hour, his concerns about his fellow players, his home and social life, and his audiences. Macready also betrays his often tortured, accusatory psychological state, his depression, and his perfectionism. Vol. II also includes a detailed account of the Astor Place Riot. Also see *Bulwer & Macready, A Chronicle of the Early Victorian Theatre* ed. Charles H. Shattuck. Urbana: University of Illinois Press, 1958.

270a. *Diaries of William Charles Macready . . .* New York: G. P. Putnam's Sons, 1912. Two Vols.

270b. *Diaries of William Charles Macready . . .* New York: Benjamin Blom, 1969. Two Vols.

270c. *The Journal of William Charles Macready, 1832-1851.* Abridged and Ed. J. C. Trewin. London: Longmans, 1967. 315 pp.

271. *Macready's Reminiscences, and Selections from His Diaries and Letters.* Ed. Sir Frederick Pollock, Bart., One of His Executors. London: Macmillan and Co., 1875. Two Vols.

These memoirs cover Macready's childhood and youth, including his father's financial difficulties as a theatre manager, and his own early schooling and appearances in country theatres. He writes of his first appearance at Covent Garden and his rise, by 1830, to a foremost place in the English theatre. He comments on the style of other actors, problems of management, public attitudes toward the theatre, the Astor Place Riot and certain non-theatrical matters such as his impressions of American character and slavery.

271a. *Macready's Reminiscences.* London: Tribner, 1875. Two Vols.

271b. *Macready's Reminiscences . . .* New ed. London: Macmillan and Co., 1876. 750 pp.

271c. *Macready's Reminiscences . . .* New York: Harper and Brothers, 1875. 721 pp.

271d. *Macready's Reminiscences . . .* New York: Harper and Brothers, 1933.

271e. *Macready's Reminiscences . . .* Extended to Seven Volumes by the Insertion of Portraits, Original Playbills, Autograph Letters and Press Cuttings. With an Introduction and Essay on Macready's Art and Character, From *The Life of Macready* by William Archer. Collected and Arranged by J. H. Leight. London: n.p., 1896. Seven Vols.

McVicker, James Hubert, 1822/24-1876.

272. *The Theatre: Its Early Days in Chicago.* A Paper Read Before the Chicago Historical Society, February 19, 1884 by J. H. McVicker. Chicago: Knight and Leonard, 1884. 88 pp.

McVicker's history of theatre in Chicago begins around 1834. The history is a personal record of his own experiences, notably his famous battle in the press with a clergyman who waged an all-out war to close down Chicago's theatres.

Maeder, Clara Fisher, 1811-1898.

273. *Autobiography of Clara Fisher Maeder*; Ed. Douglas Taylor. New York: The Dunlap Society, 1897. 138 pp.

In these rambling memoirs, Clara Fisher, once a precocious child performer in England, recites the names of her friends and bemoans the changes in her own situation and in the stage. She records her marriage to a concert manager and her career as a singer with different companies, chiefly that of her husband, James Maeder.

273a. *Autobiography . . .* New York: B. Franklin, 1970. 138 pp.

Mailbran, Maria Felicita, 1808-1836.

274. *Memoirs of the Public and Private Life of the Celebrated Madame Malibran.* London: J. Thompson, 1836. Two Vols.

These memoirs chart the Countess de Merlin's rise to prominence in the musical drama of England. They include sketches of her by her friends, selections from her correspondence and notices of her performances.

274a. *Memoirs . . .* London: H. Colburn, 1840. Two Vols.

274b. *Memoirs . . .* London: H. Colburn, 1844. Two Vols.

274c. *Memoirs . . .* Philadelphia: Carey & Hart, 1840. Two Vols.

Maltby, Henry Francis, 1880-1963.

275. *Ring up the Curtain* Being the Stage and Film Memoirs

of H. F. Maltby. With a foreword by Sir Lewis Casson. London and New York: Hutchinson, 1950. 232 pp.

Maltby was born in 1880 in South Africa. He gave up a job with the Bank of India to join a fit-up company of *The Sign and the Cross*. One chapter is devoted to this company which played fifty-one one-night stands in halls and corn exchanges. Although most of Maltby's career developed in the twentieth century, his nineteenth-century record of a young actor becoming a professional is valuable.

Mapleson, James Henry, 1830-1901.

276. *The Mapleson Memoirs 1845-1888*. New York: Bedford, and Clark Co., 1888. Two vols.

Mapleson was an impresario and manager of Italian Opera at London's Lyceum Theatre and the New York Academy of Music. His memoirs are chiefly sketches of many operatic stars of his day.

276a. *The Mapleson Memoirs . . .* 2nd Ed. London: Remington and Co., 1888. Two Vols.

276b. *The Mapleson Memoirs . . .* 3rd Ed. London: Remington and Co., 1889. Two Vols.

276c. *The Mapleson Memoirs . . .* New Ed. London: Putnam, 1966. Two Vols.

276d. *The Mapleson Memoirs . . .* New York: Appleton-Century, 1966. 346 pp.

Marbury, Elizabeth, 1856-1933.

277. *My Crystal Ball; Reminiscences* by Elizabeth Marbury. New York: Boni and Liveright, 1923. 355 pp.

Marbury worked as a playwright's agent after the death of her father forced her to support herself. She represented both American and French playwrights at a time when translations of French plays were extremely popular in America. Among her clients were Victorien Sardou and Oscar Wilde.

277a. *My Crystal Ball . . .* New York: Boni and Liveright, 1924. 355 pp.

Marchesi, Blanche, 1895-1933

278. *Singer's Pilgrimage*. London: G. Richards Co., 1923. 304 pp.

Marchesi, a dramatic soprano, first trained as a violinist with Mikisch in Germany and with Colonne in Paris. Her study as a singer began under the direction of her mother, Mathilde Marchesi, whose assistant she was for many years. She made her debut in 1895 in Berlin. She writes of singing Wagner at Covent Garden and of her tours of Russia, Central Europe, and the United States.

278a. *Singer's Pilgrimage*. New York: Arno Press, 1977. 304 pp.

278b. *Singer's Pilgrimage*. New York: Da Capo Press, 1978. 304 pp.

Maretzek, Max, 1821-1897.

279. *Crochets and Quavers, or Revelations of an Opera Manager in America*. New York: Samuel French, 1855. 346 pp.

Maretzek, a composer and opera manager, came to the United States in 1848 from his studies in Vienna. His memoirs begin in this year with his position as conductor and manager of the Italian Opera Company in New York. The memoirs are in the form of open letters to prominent musical friends about the American character, opera repertory, theatre audiences, the Astor Place Riot and the Macready-Forrest feud.

279a. *Crochets and Quavers . . .* American Culture Series. Ann Arbor: University Microfilms, 1956. 346 pp.

279b. *Crochets and Quavers . . .* in *Revelations of an Opera Singer in Nineteenth Century America*. New York: Dover Publications, 1968. 346 pp. Includes *Sharps and Flats*.

280. *Sharps and Flats*. New York: American Music Publishing Co., 1890. 86 pp.

Maretzek describes his memoirs as "a serio-comic history of opera in America for the last forty years, with reminiscences and anecdotes of artists, maestros, impresarios, journalists, patrons, stockholders and other dead heads . . . ." He has chapters on Alboni, Sontag, the Academy of Music, and opera in Havanna and Mexico.

280a. *Sharps and Flats* in *Revelations of an Opera Singer in Nineteenth Century America*. New York: Dover Publications, 1968. 87 pp.

Markham, Pauline, 1847-1919.

281. *The Life of Pauline Markham* written by herself. New York: n.p. 1871. 31 pp.

This is reportedly the account of a young actress who quits the company of Lydia Thompson, playing at Wood's Museum, to join the cast of *The Black Crook*. The book is concerned with one subject only: the suitors, or "spoons," or stage-door johnnies who feed her ego at the same time they make her life miserable. There is nothing here about other aspects of theatre life.

Marston, John Westland, 1819-1890.

282. *Our Recent Actors; Being Recollections Critical and in Many Instances Personal of Late Distinguished Performers of Both Sexes.* With Some Incidental Notices of Living Actors by Westland Marston. London: S. Low, Marston Searle and Rivington, 1888. Two Vols.

Marston, a playwright, not only studies the most prominent actors of his time, including Charles Kemble, the Keans, Macready and Madame Vestris, he also reveals something of the working relationship between playwright and actor. For example, he details a disagreement between himself and Charles Kean, who wanted to alter the ending of a play written by Marston.

282a. *Our Recent Actors* . . . London: S. Low, Marston Searle and Rivington, 1898. 392 pp.

Massett, Stephen C., 1820-1898.

283. *What "Jeems Pipes of Pipesville" Saw-And-Did Drifting About.* New York: Carelton, 1863. 371 pp.

Stephen C. Massett, a British-born actor, moved to the United States in 1837. He found his way to San Francisco in 1849; thus his work is a rich source of information about the pioneer theatre in the far west, including performances in mining camps.

283a. *What Jeems . . . Saw-And-Did.* Louisville, Kentucky: Lost Cause Press, 1970. 371 pp.

283b. *What Jeems . . . Saw-And-Did.* American Fiction Series. Ann Arbor, Michigan: University Microfilms, 1971. 371 pp.

Mathews, Charles James, 1803-1878.

284. *The Life of Charles James Mathews Chiefly Autobiographical With Selections From His Correspondence and Speeches.* Ed. Charles Dickens. With Portraits. London: Macmillan and Co., 1879. Two Vols.

After his death, the autobiographical papers of Charles Mathews were edited by Charles Dickens at the request of Mathews' family. Dickens has chosen papers that reveal something of Mathews' early life and education, his first appearance on stage in a private theatrical, journeys to Italy, Wales and Venice, and his subsequent decision to devote his life to the theatre.

Occasional details are provided about the many theatres in Hawaii, Australia and India in which he appeared. The final chapter is an evaluation of his career.

284a. *The Life of Charles James Mathews* . . . New York: Harper and Row, 1879. 85 pp.

285. *Memoirs of Charles Mathews, Comedian* by Mrs. Mathews. London: Richard Bentley, 1838. Four Vols.

Volume One opens with an autobiographical fragment exclusively about the eighteenth century. Mathew's random notes are scattered throughout the rest of the volumes, all written by Mrs. Mathews.

Mathews, John, n.d.

286. *Bow! Wow!! Wow!!! Life and Theatrical Career of John Mathews, Champion Swordsman, Showman, Dogman and Pantomimist In Which Will be Truthfully Depicted the Trying Events and Sensational Situations of Forty-Five Years in Sixty Theatre Royals, Eighty Minor Theatres, Twenty Circuses, Twenty Gardens, One Hundred Music Hall, Thirty Concert Rooms, Fifty Booths, Forty Fairs, Fourteen Penny Dukeys, Eight Yaffs . . . as Dog-man, Training Thirty Dogs. Career in Theatrical Life as Proprietor, Stage Manager, Leading Actor, Dog Star, Juvenile Man, Heavy Man . . . Pantomimist, Utility, Prompter, Stage Carpenter, Property Master, Gas Director, Pyrotechnist, Supermaster, and Bill Inspector*. London, n.p. 1874. Four Vols.

One of the most revealing aspects of Mathews' career is that at the extraordinarily young age of fourteen, he played leading roles in a juvenile touring company called a "Penny Dukey" production. He also had experience in extempore performance, in the manner of the *comedia del arte*. As an adult he appeared in a series of variety acts--equestrian, aquatic, canine, pantomime--rendered at Astley's and similar theatres in Brighton, Portsmouth, Leeds and other key cities in the provinces.

286a. *Bow! Wow!! Wow!!!* . . . London: J. Bursill, 1876. Four Vols.

286b. *Bow! Wow!! Wow!!!* . . . London: n.p.., 187?. 15 pp.

Matthews, Alfred Edward, 1869-1960.

287. *Matty; An Autobiography*. With a Foreword by Noel Coward. London: Hutchinson, 1952. 232 pp.

Matthews' first job was that of call-boy in the Princess' Theatre, Oxford Street. At sixteen he became an actor, making one of the first theatrical tours ever allowed in South Africa. Back in England he joined a fit-up, and later toured with Charles Hawtry's Company in *The Private Secretary*. His travel experiences are extensive, and he writes of South African audiences, Kimberley, deBeers diamond mines, and Zulus. He devotes his final chapter to an estimate of the theatre in general at the end of the century.

Maude, Cyril, 1862-1951.

288. *Behind the Scenes With Cyril Maude by Himself*. London: J. Murray, 1927. 331 pp.

Maude, and English actor and manager, made his theatrical debut in America. Sent by his family to work on a Canadian farm in New York, he instead got a job in a touring company managed by the German tragedian, Daniel Bandmann. Maude's description of this wretched crew and his own strange contract, without salary, is the most interesting part of the book. Eventually he achieved success as an actor in the company of Charles Wyndham and as a manager in partnership with Fredrick Harrison. A large part of the book is, literally, a remembrance of old times and old faces: the season of 1897 and J. M. Barrie's *The Little Minister* and *The Black Tulip* in 1898, and older revivals in 1900. He lists casts and mentions many people with whom he worke

288a. *Lest I Forget; Being Reminiscences of Social and Dramatic Life in England and America* by Cyril Maude Illustrated. New York: J. H. Dears, 1928. This is the New York edition of *Behind the Scenes*.

Mayer, Sylvain, 1863-1948.

289. *Reminiscences of a K. C. Theatrical and Legal* by Sylvain Mayer. London: Selwyn and Blout, 1924. 197 pp.

Sylvain Mayer grew up in a stage atmosphere: his father was a journalist, theatre manager, and play adapter. Mayer discusses his youth as his father's assistant at the Princess Theatre in Oxford Street and his own development as a dramatist.

Meade, Ed., 1863-

290. *Doubling Back, Autobiography of an Actor, Serio-comical* by Edwards Hoag Meade. Containing Plain Anecdotes of the Stage, How I Became an Actor, and the Result, Stories While Barnstorming, and Some Original Verse, Illustrated by Vade Garton. Chicago: Hammond Press, W. B. Conkey and Co., 1916. 180 pp.

Meade wrote this account of his career as a comedian and comic impersonator after suffering a disabling stroke. Most of his life was spent working in rural areas with companies that were always on the verge of disintegration. He also appeared with the Oakes Swiss

Bell Ringers. The book shows the vicissitudes of old-time barnstorming, which required actors to play in such improvised theatres as butcher-shops and forced them to take up other jobs periodically to make a living.

Melba, Nellie, 1854-1931.

291. *Melodies and Memories* by Nellie Melba. London: T. Butterworth, 1925. 335 pp.

Melba writes of her youth in Australia, study in Paris, debuts in London and Paris and tours of America. Her other subjects are American hostesses, the Prince of Wales, American audiences and Sarah Bernhardt, from whom she had make-up and acting lessons. She claims to deplore the commerical exploitation of stars; in her case it involved the marketing of "Peach Melba" without her permission.

291a. *Melodies and Memories* . . . New York: George H. Doran Co., 1926. 339 pp.

291b. *Melodies and Memories*. AMS Press, 1971. 339 pp.

291c. *Melodies and Memories*. Freeport, N.Y.: Books for Libraries Press, 1970. 339 pp.

Melford, Mark, -1914.

292. *Life in a Booth*. London: Henderson, 1913. 258 pp.

Melford writes light-heartedly of his hard life in a booth theatre, concentrating on the eccentrics, the poverty, the landlords, the thwarted ambition, and the audiences. He ends, somewhat beside the point, with an appeal for women's suffrage.

Mendle, Lady Elsie. See de Wolfe, Elsie.

Merivale, Herman Charles, 1839-1906.

293. *Bar, Stage, and Platforms; Autobiographic Memories* by Herman Charles Merivale. With a Portrait. London: Chatto and Windus, 1902. 304 pp.

Merivale records the society surrounding stage and bar in the sixties and seventies by describing several figures prominent in each profession. He offers material on his own plays, specifically *The Oxford Don*, on Edmund Kean, whom his grandfather had encouraged, and actors Charles Kean and Charles Fechter. He also describes the educational system in England.

Merlin, Maria. See Malibran, Maria Felicita.

Michael, Edward, 1853-1950.

294. *Tramps of a Scamp* by Edward Michael in Collaboration with J. B. Booth. London: T. Werner Laurie, 1928. 211 pp.

Michael, a theatrical business manager, writes a free-wheeling narrative account of sailing in the Pacific, life in the far west, a soap factory, the Comstock Lode and miscellaneous theatre experiences. Several chapters are devoted to Grand Opera and two to Lily Langtry. Other chapters are on yachting, Fleet Street and his booking agency's methods.

Middleton, George, 1846-1926.

295. *Circus Memories; Reminiscences of George Middleton* As Told to and Written by his Wife. Los Angeles: G. Rice and Sons, Printers, 1913. 118 pp.

Middleton joined the circus as a young man and followed the same profession for over forty years, traveling over the midwest and upper south and as far west as Salt Lake City. He worked with circus men of prominence, including Adam Forepaugh, James A. Bailey, W. W. Cole, Blondine the Tightrope Walker and James Robinson the rider. He writes of all of them as well as circus "curiosities": fat ladies, ossified men, two-headed singers, the Chinese Giant and tatooed men.

Miller, David Prince, 1808-1873.

296. *The Life of Miller, The Showman.* Glasgow: n.p., 1942. 140 pp.

As a young boy trying to feed himself, Miller came upon a theatrical company performing in a barn, just minutes before its members were deserted by the manager. Miller, a complete neophyte, took over the company's management and failed. He was more successful at playing con-games with cups and cards. Even while he was a young man, however, he put together his own traveling stock company and built a theatre in Glasgow. Although in his several managerial endeavours he was able to hire actors of the calibre of Fanny Kemble, Macready, Phelps and Glover, he failed repeatedly. His book concludes with an explanation of magic tricks.

296a. *The Life of a Showman To Which is Added Managerial Struggles* . . . London: T. H. Lacy; Leeds: C. A. Wilson and Co., 1849. 192 pp.

296b. *The Life of a Showman; And the Managerial Struggles of David Prince Miller: With Anecdotes and Letters of Some of the Most Celebrated Modern Actors and Actresses. The Art of Fortune Telling. An Expose of the Practices of Begging*

Imposters, Mountebanks, Jugglers, and Various Deceivers of the Public; Together With the Secrets of Conjuring, and an Explanation of the Most Celebrated and Striking Tricks of Wizards and Conjurers. 2nd Ed. *With Considerable Additions.* London: Thomas Hailes Lacy, 1849. 192 pp.

296c. *The Life of a Showman* . . . London: E. Avery, 1849. 192 pp.

296d. *The Life of a Showman* . . . London: T. H. Lacy, 1853. 192 pp.

296e. *The Life of a Showman* . . . London: T. H. Lacy, 1860. 192 pp.

296f. *The Life of a Showman* . . . London: E. Avery, 1880. 192 pp.

Millward, Jessie, 1861-1932.

297. *Myself and Others* by Jessie Millward in Collaboration with J. B. Booth. With Eighteen Illustrations. London: Hutchinson and Co., 1923. 318 pp.

> Millward is an example of an actress who made her professional debut in a speaking role and continued to be active professionally for most of her life. She writes of acting with Mrs. Kendall and Henry Irving at the Lyceum and of her friendship with William Terriss, who died in her arms.

297a. *Myself and Others.* 2nd Ed. Boston: Small, Maynard and Co., 1924. 318 pp.

Miln, Louise Jordan, 1864-1933.

298. *When We Were Strolling Players in the East* by Louise Jordan Miln. New York: Charles Scribner's Sons, 1894. 354 pp.

> Although Louise Jordan Miln was an actress, married to an actor, the memoirs of her theatrical tour are altogether about the eastern cultures she encountered, not about the theatre. She is particularly interested in the family structure, social customs, and clothing of the Chinese, Japanese and Eastern Indians in the nineteenth century.

298a. *When We Were Strolling Players* . . . London: G. Bell and Sons, 1895. 354 pp.

298b. *When We Were Strolling Players* . . . New York: Charles Scribner's Sons, 1896. 354 pp.

Modjeska, Helena, 1840/44-1909.

299. *Memories and Impressions of Helena Modjeska; An Autobiography.* New York: The Macmillan Co., 1910. 571 pp.

Modjeska gives an account of her girlhood and the artists' community she knew in Poland. She left in 1876 for California. Although she was already an established star on the European stage, she required months of training in English before she was able to appear on the American stage. Thereafter she toured the mining camps of the West, the east, the midwest and completed an engagement in London. Her famous parts included Shakespearean heroines, Camille, and Nora in Ibsen's *The Doll's House.*

299a. *Memories and Impressions* . . . New York: Benjamin Blom, 1969. 571 pp.

Molony, Kitty, n.d.

300. *Behind the Scenes with Edwin Booth* by Katherine Goodale (Kitty Molony) with a foreword by Mrs. Fiske. Boston and New York: Houghton Mifflin Co., 1931. 327 pp.

Kitty Molony's autobiographical account of her employment in the companies of Lawrence Barrett and Edwin Booth provides rare glimpses of the production crew, costuming, and properties as well as the expected character study of Edwin Booth.

300a. *Behind the Scenes with Edwin Booth.* London and New York: Benjamin Blom, 1969. 327 pp.

Moore, Eva, 1870-1955.

301. *Exits and Entrances* by Eva Moore with Twenty Illustrations. London: Chapman and Hall, 1923. 259 pp.

Only the first four chapters of Eva Moore's memoirs are pertinent to a study of the nineteenth century. In that portion of the book she deals with her childhood in Brighton, her career as a dancing teacher (Winston Churchill was one of her first pupils), amateur theatricals, the thunderous objections which her parents made to her going on the stage, and her success in London, where she became a member of Charles Hawtrey's company.

301a. *Exits and Entrances.* New York: Stokes Co., 1923. 259 pp.

Morosco, Oliver, 1875/6-1945.

302. *The Oracle of Broadway.* Written From his Own Notes and Comments by Helen M. Morosco and Leonard Paul Dugger. Caldwell, Idaho: The Caxton Printers, Inc., 1914. 391 pp.

Morosco tells a story of San Francisco and other Western Mining communities in the last two decades of the century. The child of itinerant show people, he became a performer in minstrel shows and circuses when he was a youth. Although his irresponsible father frequently placed a heavy burden on Morosco by abruptly leaving the young boy with the full responsibility of the family, he was a show business wizard and young Oliver's ticket into show management.

Morris, Clara, 1846/48/49-1925.

303. *The Life of a Star* by Clara Morris. New York: McClure, Phillips and Co., 1906. 363 pp.

Morris's third book containing memoirs, actually a continuation of the first, reports on her courtship and wedding. She also tells random stories about a foolish ingenue, Augustin Daly's direction, pretty and ugly actresses, Henry Bergh, founder of the ASPCA, James A. Garfield, William McKinley and Dion Boucicault. Two of her chapters are bitter attacks on Mormonism as being vicious, dangerous and demeaning to women.

304. *Life on the Stage; My Personal Experiences and Recollections*. New York: McClure, Phillips and Co., 1901. 399 pp.

Morris writes about her poverty-stricken childhood and, much to her mother's horror, her first engagement as a ballet girl. She recounts her rise through the ranks from ballet girl to utility actress to juvenile leads, first in the small companies of the midwest, then in the New York companies of Augustin Daly and A. M. Palmer. One section is devoted to John Wilkes Booth, whom she and her company had admired both personally and professionally.

304a. *Life on the Stage* . . . New York: McClure, Phillips and Co., 1902. 399 pp.

305. *Stage and Confidences, Talks About Players, and Play-acting* by Clara Morris. Boston: Lothrop Publishing Co., 1902. 316 pp.

Stage Confidences is a book of advice to the stage-struck girl, advice couched in the continual anecdotes and memoirs of Morris' life. Her approach is to indicate what the true nature of the stage is, the hard work, its failure to satisfy all comers, its lack of romance, and then to indicate its reasonable rewards, considerable for a woman living in an age of occupational limitation. It remains one of the best sources of information on young women in the nineteenth-century American theatre.

Morris, Felix, 1850-1900.

306. *Reminiscences* by Felix Morris. New York: International Telegram Co., 1892. 176 pp.

Morris illustrates the almost sterotypical portrait of the struggling actor. Abandoning the study of medicine for the stage, he came to America, where he endured hard times, landed a job as head "super" in Albany, New York, and ultimately met with success in New York City and London.

Morton, William, 1838-1938.

307. *I Remember (A Feat of Memory)* by William Morton, His life's career from infancy, embracing nearly a century. With Twenty-nine Illustrations. Hull: Goddard, Walker and Braun, Printers, 1934. 173 pp.

Morton, once a printer's devil and journalist, turned to show business as an advance agent and manager of Morton's Greenwich Theatre. He has information on spiritualists and illusionists with whom he had close association, on the Fenian Riots in Ireland, on London music halls, and on some of the celebrities he knew: Henry Irving, George Grossmith, and others.

Mott, Edward Spencer, 1844-1910

308. *A Mingled Yard. The Autobiography of E. S. Mott.* London: E. Arnold, 1898. 348 pp.

A professional soldier for most of his life, Edward Spencer Mott, on the verge of starvation after his separation from the army, considered several professions before deciding on the stage. His career was very brief, but he writes of his fondness for the stage, the tricks used by the old comedians to upstage each other and the routine of rehearsals. In addition to memoirs of the theatre and the military, he concludes with chapters on horse racing.

Mowatt, Anna Cora, 1819-1870.

309. *Autobiography of an Actress; or Eight Years on the Stage.* by Anna Cora Mowatt. Boston: Ticknor, Reed and Fields, 1853. 448 pp.

Mowatt, a professional writer of some reputation as well as an outstanding actress, records the unusual circumstances of her entry on the stage and her long battle with physical ailments and financial disaster, both of which were alleviated in some degree by mesmerism and her stage career. As one who had been a writer and a newcomer to the stage, Mowatt has a good notion of those professional secrets about which an audience would be curious: rehearsals, make-up, costuming, and touring.

Mozart, George, 1864-1947.

310. *Limelight*. London: Hurst and Blackett, 1938. 284 pp.

Mozart began his career as a drummer in the Theatre Royal, Yarmouth. He soon became a clown, a bandmaster and a minstrel comedian in music halls and circuses. Off and on he was a pantomimist in several variety shows while, at the same time, trying to support his family at different times by running a pub, a tobacco shop, and a hair dressing establishment. Even though a wished-for chance to perform at Drury Lane fell through, he did achieve some successes at the Oxford, the Tivoli and the Pavillion. His memoir is particularly useful for its character sketches of music hall entertainers.

Murdock, James E., 1811-1893.

311. *The Stage, or, Recollections of Actors and Acting From an Experience of Fifty Years; a Series of Dramatic Sketches* by James E. Murdock. With an Appendix. Philadelphia: J. M. Stoddard and Co., 1880. 510 pp.

Murdock shows more interest in theories of acting than do many of his fellow actor-writers. His beginning chapters include discussions of schools of acting, mimicry and imitation, voice, reading, and mannerisms. Very little of the book is personal memoirs, but he stresses repeatedly that his judgments and many of his anecdotes are based on personal experience.

311a. *The Stage* . . . Cincinnati: Robert Clarke, 1884. 510 pp.

311b. *The Stage* . . . New York: Benjamin Blom, 1969. 510 pp.

N

Navarro, Mary, see Anderson, Mary.

Neilson, Julia, 1869-1957.

312. *This For Remembrance.* London: Hurst and Co., 1940. 259 pp.

> Julia Neilson found her way into the theatre by way of the Royal Academy of Music and an introduction to William S. Gilbert. As a singer-actress, she performed chiefly with Gilbert, but also with H. Beerbohm Tree at the Haymarket. She writes a separate chapter on Fred Terry, her husband, and also provides one of the very few intimate pictures of the home life, marriage and children of the actress.

312a. *This For Remembrance* . . . Third Impression. London: Hurst and Blackett, 1941. 259 pp.

Newton, Henry Chance, 1854-1931.

313. *Cues and Curtain Calls; Being the Theatrical Reminiscences of H. Chance Newton* ("Carados" of *The Referee*) With Introduction by Sir Johnston Forbes-Robertson and Fifty-Six Illustrations. London: John Lane, 1927. 306 pp.

> Newton, a player, playwright and critic, writes extensively about the theatre, drawing from his experiences with Henry Irving and Irving's sons, H. B. and Lawrence, Beerbohn Tree and Wilson Barrett. He focuses on two other mattters: a comparison of several different interpretations of Hamlet by actors and the contribution of Jewish men and women to the theatre.

314. *Idols of the "Halls," Being My Music Hall Memories* by H. Chance Newton "Carados" of *The Referee.* With a Foreword by Sir Oswald Stoll. London: Heath Cranston, 1928. 256 pp.

This is one of the most complete first-hand histories of London's music halls--its various theatrical homes, its comic male singers, its female stars, its managers, ventriloquists, magicians, and song writers. From his youth Newton played in "transformed pubs" and moved on in his mature years to the large well-heeled Empire, Palace and Hippodrome.

Nobles, Milton, 1847-1924.

315. *Milton Nobles' "Shop Talk." Stage Stories, Anecdotes of the Theatre, Reminiscences.* Milwaukee: Riverside Printing Co., 1889. 205 pp.

Milton Nobles, a stage manager who went to California to act and dig for gold, was, despite his dreams of wealth, in poverty for most of his life. His memoirs consist of information about stage promotion, combination shows, and parodies of stage characters: the women who rise to stardom instantly and then retire to teach elocution, stage aspirants and theatre reformers.

315a. *Milton Nobles' "Shop Talk"* Milwaukee: n.p., 188?. 205 pp.

Nugent, John Charles, 1878-1947.

316. *Its a Great Life* by J. C. Nugent. New York: The Dial Press, 1940. 331 pp.

Nugent, an actor and dramatist, gives an excellent portrayal of his own early years in show business in the nineteenth century in a series of small-time dramatic companies barnstorming across the hinterlands. He chronicles the weary monotony of one-night stands, the apathy of many old professionals, and the gimmicks used for advertising. He also shows his own introduction to the New York stage and vaudeville and his emergence as a successful playwright. Nugent was among the vaudeville performers who waged protests against managers in "The White Rats of America" organization.

P~Q

Pack, James, n.d.

317. *Some Account of the Life and Experience of James Pack late celebrated actor, in the Pantomime Department, at Theatre Royal, Drury Lane, and Other Places: But Now, by the Grace of God, a Disciple and Follower of the Lord Jesus Christ.* In a Series of Letters Written by Himself, and Addressed to Mr. Henry Paice, Pastor of the Particular Baptist Church, Meeting in Lewisham Street, Westminster. London: the author, 1819. 45 pp.

> This minister is a converted actor who found the traveling theatres and circus companies he worked with to be cruel (like slave-drivers) and sacrilegious (they travelled on Sunday). He became wealthy and successful in London, he claims, before his conversion ended all performing.

Parke, William Thomas, 1762-1847.

318. *Musical Memories; Comprising an Account of the General State of Music in England, from the first Commemoration of Handel, in 1784, to the year 1830. Interspersed with Numerous Anecdotes, Musical, Histrionic* . . . by W. T. Parke, Forty Years Principal Oboist to the Theatre Royal Covent Garden. London: Henry Colburn and Richard Bentley, 1830. Two Vols.

> This is a year-by-year chronicle of musical theatre in England written by a man who was for forty years principal oboist at the Theatre Royal, Covent Garden. It is primarily made up of anecdotes, theatre schedules and lists of stars. He closes with a state-of-the-theatre commentary.

318a. *Musical Memories* . . . New York: Da Capo Press, 1970. Two Vols. in One.

Parker, Louis Napoleon, 1852-1944.

319. *Several of my Lives* by Louis N. Parker. With Many Illustrations. London: Chapman and Hall, 1928. 312 pp.

Parker writes of a boyhood spent in several European cities and of the training he received at the Royal Academy of Music. For nineteen years he worked as a school master and composer and dates his theatrical life from 1886, at which time he left his post at Sherburne school and came to London to begin a career as a playwright.

319a. *Some of My First Nights* by Louis Napoleon Parker. London: Chiswick Press, 1914. 46 pp.

In a small privately printed book, Parker facetiously relates the abysmal failure of his first few opening nights as a playwright.

Parry, John Orlando, 1810-1879.

320. *Victorian Swansdown. Extracts From the Early Travel Diaries of John Orlando Parry, the Victorian Entertainer.* ed. Cyril Bruyn Andrews and J. A. Orr-Ewing. London: John Murray, 1935. 244 pp.

During his lifetime Parry was a singer, music critic, composer, editor, manager, clown, impersonator and burlesque comedian. He soon found that the concert hall and concert tour were more to his liking than the stage. Parry is more intrigued by and interested in writing about his contacts with titled gentry in England and on the continent than he is in writing of his life on stage.

320a. *Victorian Swansdown . . .* London: John Murray, 1935. 244 pp.

Parsons, Samuel, 1762-

321. *Poetical Trifles, Being a Collection of Songs, and Fugitive Pieces* by S. Parsons, Late of the Theatre Royal, York, With a Sketch of the Life of the Author. York: R. Johnson, 1822. 66 pp.

Although Parsons joined a group of comedians in 1784, he immediately detested his job and felt trapped by the investment he had made in his wardrobe. He toured in several English theatrical circuits in a short time, settling finally in one where he spent ten years. He claims to be cursed by misfortune and poverty and, at the time he writes his book, is out of work and out of luck as usual.

Paterson, Peter, 1824-1892.

322. *The Confessions of a Strolling Player: or Three Years' Experience in Theatres Rural.* London: Bertram

and Company, 1852. 42 pp.

Paterson's memoirs, a warning to stage-struck youth, end with the admonition, "Don't go on the stage!" Ironically, however, the story of his failure is more revealing of the everyday workings of circus, strolling companies, and booths than are the memoirs of successful actors.

322a. *Behind the Scenes: Being the Confessions of a Strolling Player* . . . Edinburgh: D. Mathers; Glasgow: W. Lowe, 1858. 166 pp.

To *The Confessions* Paterson adds a body of correspondence and a few more reminiscences of other actors.

322b. *Behind the Scenes.* Edinburgh: D. Mathers, 1859. 166 pp.

322c. *Glimpses of Real Life as Seen in the Theatrical World and in Bohemia: Being the Confessions of Peter Paterson, a Strolling Comedian.* Another Enlarged Edition. Edinburgh: William P. Nimmo, 1864. 352 pp.

322d. *Glimpses of Real Life* . . . Hamden, Conn.: Archon Books, 1979. 352 pp.

Peile, Kinsey, 1862-1934.

323. *Candied Peel. Tales Without Prejudice* by Kinsey Peile. London: A. & C. Black, 1931. 251 pp.

After a career as a professional soldier, Kinsey Peile launched his stage career by hiring his own playwright and composer to write a vehicle especially for him, then renting a theatre in which to appear. His effort led to success, a music hall career, and a life-long association with stars of such prominence as Lily Langtry and Sarah Bernhardt.

Penley, William Sidney, 1851/52-1912.

324. *Penley on Himself. The Confession of a Conscientious Artist.* Bristol: J. W. Arrowsmith; London: Simpkin, Marshall, Hamilton, Kent and Co., 1896. 196 pp.

After being thrown out of a monastery when he was a young man, Penley made a career for himself at the Royalty Theatre, the Globe, and the Gaiety. His most famous role, almost a profession in itself, was that of Charley's Aunt. The memoirs show a strong interest in Gilbert and Sullivan, sports, gambling and private clubs.

Pennington, W. H., 1832-1923.

325. *Sea, Camp, and Stage; Incidents in the Life of a*

Survivor of the Balaclava Light Brigade. Briston: J. W. Arrowsmith, 1906. 200 pp.

Pennington wrote briefly of Balaclava and related numerous anecdotes concerning himself and his friends. His memoir, which contains much about the military and very little about the stage, has the tone of a fireside chat, a series of tales related by an old trooper.

Philips, F. C., 1849-1921.

326. *My Varied Life.* London: Eveleigh Nash, 1914. 335 335 pp.

Philips' "Varied" life included his being a soldier, theatre manager, member of the bar, journalist, novelist and dramatist. He discusses the advantages of each as a profession. The theatrical professional, he writes, must come to terms with censorship, the vicissitudes of management, poor salaries, public taste, and the necessity of advertising.

Phillips, Henry, 1801-1876.

327. *Musical and Personal Recollections During Half a Century.* London: Skeet, 1864. Two Vols.

Phillips entered his profession as a member of choruses and processions. After a frightening period during which he almost lost his voice, he began to achieve some reputation in private theatricals, clubs, and churches. As a performer who could render both popular and classical music, his contacts among musicians were extensive.

Pinero, Arthur Wing, 1855-1934.

328. *The Collected Letters of Arthur Wing Pinero.* Ed. J. P. Wearing. Minneapolis: University of Minnesota Press, 1974. 302 pp.

Pinero, in letters to theatrical and literary friends, comments on censorship,the state of the English stage, French and German drama, and his own plays and career.

Pitou, Augustus, 1843-1915.

329. *Masters of the Show. As Seen in Retrospection by One Who Has Been Associated with the American Stage for Nearly Fifty Years* by Augustus Pitou. New York: The Neale Publishing Co., 1914. 186 pp.

Pitou's first role was under the management of Edwin Booth in 1867. Pitou includes a letter in which Booth evaluates his talents and prospects as an actor and advises Pitou that he will never be great or achieve beyond his present level. Whether because of this or not, Pitou turned from acting to stage management. His memoirs reveal much about Edwin Booth, Edwin Forrest, and the change in theatre management in the 1880s and 90s, particularly the growth of combinations and, later, the syndicate.

329a. *Masters of the Show*. . . New York: Thomas Y. Crowell Co., 1914.

Planche, James Robinson, 1796-1880.

330. *The Recollections and Reflections of J. R. Planche. A Professional Autobiography*. London: Tinsley Brothers, 1872. Two Vols.

Planche gives a year-by-year account of his theatrical career as a playwright and manager. He wrote some 196 pieces for the theatre, produced opera, drama, and burlesque, and traveled extensively in the continent. As an antiquarian, Planche also wrote a book on the history of British costume.

330a. *The Recollections and Reflections*. . . New and Revised Ed. London: Sampson Low, Marston and Co., 1901. Two Vols.

Pond, Major J. B., 1838-1903.

331. *Eccentricities of a Genius. Memories of Famous Men and Women of the Platform and Stage* by Major J. B. Pond. New York: G. W. Dillingham Co., 1900. 546 pp.

Major Pond, a pioneer settler of Wisconsin, marched with John Brown in 1856. He exchanged his military career for a theatrical one when he was hired by the Redpath booking agency. The book is essentially a memory of some eighty-five people he came to know after managing their appearances on tour. Among the most successful performers he remembers are Ralph Waldo Emerson and Mark Twain. His book concludes with a "survey of the Lyceum Field."

331a. *Eccentricities of a Genius* . . . London: Chatto and Windus, 1901. 364 pp.

Poole, John, 1786/92-1872.

332. *Sketches and Recollections*. London: Published for H. Colburn by Richard Bentley, 1835. Two Vols.

Poole's *Sketches* are more anecdotal than narrative. He reveals how he lost a family inheritance after an aunt, to whom he had devoted his life left all her money to public charity. Volume Two includes "Notes for a Memoir," more whimsical and amusing than informative. Poole wrote for both Drury Lane and the Haymarket. *Hamlet Travestie*, finished in 1810, was his most renowned achievement and his first published work.

Power, Tyrone, 1795-1841.

333. *Impressions of America During the Years 1833, 1834, and 1835* by Tyrone Power, Esq. London: Richard Bentley, 1836. Two Vols.

Power, an Irish actor playing in America, observes Yankee character and cities, comparing British and American audiences, actors and methods of rehearsing. He is interested in American prisons, American Indians, factories, Southern cities and the Southern temperament.

333a. *Impressions of America . . .* Philadelphia: Carey, Lea and Blanchard, 1836. Two Vols.

333b. *Impressions of America . . .* 2nd American ed. Philadelphia: Carey, Lea and Blanchard, 1836. Two Vols. in One.

333c. *Impressions of America . . .* American Culture Series Ann Arbor: University Microfilms, 1966. Two Vols.

333d. *Impressions of America . . .* New York: Benjamin Blom, 1971. Two Vols. in One.

Powers, James T., 1862-1943.

334. *Twinkle Little Star. Sparkling Memories of Seventy Years* by James T. Power. With a Foreword by Charles Hanson Towne, With Over One Hundred Illustrations. New York: G. P. Putnam's Sons, 1939. 379 pp.

Powers began as a singer, dancer, and acrobat in humble music halls, beer gardens and circuses. He graduated to light opera at Drury Lane Theatre and as a regular member of Augustin Daly's company. He provides the reader with pictures of Broadway and the Bowery, including fashions and customs in the 1870s and 80s.

Quinn, Germaine, n.d.

335. *Fifty Years Backstage, Being the Life Story of a Theatrical Mechanic* by Germaine Quinn. Minneapolis: Stage Publishing Co., 1926. 204 pp.

Quinn writes a who's who of entertainment arranged in categories of stars, magicians, musicians and vaudevillians. Most interesting are his accounts of his first introduction to back-stage life as the basket boy at the Minneapolis Opera House, his concluding defense of the drama, and his account of the formation of unions in Minneapolis theatres in the last three decades of the nineteenth century.

R

Randall, Harry, 1860-1932.

336. *Harry Randall, Old Time Comedian* by Himself; With a Foreword by Charles B. Cochran. London: S. Low, Marston and Co., 191-. 242 pp.

> Randall made his first appearance in 1871 in a Drury Lane pantomime. He worked as a supporting player in the 1880s in London music halls and private concerts, having to do comic female impersonations until he achieved star status. His memoir is particularly valuable for its insights into the methods of comedians, and how they could work for or against each other.

336a. *Harry Randall* . . . London: S. Low, Marston and Co., 1930. 242 pp.

Ranous, Dora Knowlton, 1859-1916.

337. *Diary of a Daly Debutante, Being Passages from the Journal of a Member of Augustin Daly's Famous Company of Players*. New York: Duffield and Co., 1910. 249 pp.

> This diary, published from a manuscript, became publically available about 20 years after it was written. Though the author is not named on the publication, she has been identified as Dora Ranous. The subject is a single company: its rehearsals, back-stage activity, personnel, and tours.

337a. *Diary of a Daly Debutante* . . . New York: Benjamin Blom, 1972. 249 pp.

Reeder, Louise, 1837-1859.

338. *Currer Lyle: or The Stage in Romance and the Stage in Reality* by Louise Reeder. New York: E. D. Long, 1850. 361 pp.

The authenticity of this memoir is decidedly suspicious. It is presented as Louise Reeder's account of villainous deceptions, seductions and betrayals on the part of actors, managers and stage-door mashers.

338a. *Currer Lyle . . .* Philadelphia: T. B. Peterson, 1857. 361 pp.

Reeve, Ada, 1876-1966.

339. *Take it For a Fact; A Record of My Years on the Stage*. With a Foreword by Sir Coompton Mackenzie. Illustrated with the Raymond Mander and Joe Mitchenson Theatre Collection. London: Heinemann, 1954. 263 pp.

Ada Reeve, reared in a family of actors, first appeared on stage at five years old in a minor role and held a position in a stock company as a child. Her first major role was Little Willie in *East Lynn.* Male juvenile roles continued to be her specialty until, in 1886, her music hall career began. She is an example of the child, like the more famous Lotta Crabtree, who supported a large family of brothers and sisters, often working three and four music halls a night, changing costumes on route. Throughout her marriage and the rearing of two children, she continued to act in both music halls and legitimate theatres.

Reeve, Wybert, 1831-1906.

340. *From Life.* Selected and republished by Request From *The Australian* and Other Journals. London: G. Robertson, 1891. 248 pp.

Reeve describes himself as an actor, writer, manager and traveller. His accounts of Charles Mathews, Joe Jefferson, Rachel and Charles Kean come from his own knowledge of them, but he offers little information about his own life.

340a. *From Life . . .* London: F. V. White and Co., 1892. 248 pp.

Reeves, John Sims, 1818/22-1900.

341. *Sims Reeves. His Life and Recollections* written by himself. London: Simpkin, Marshall and Co., and the London Music Publishing Co., 1888. 279 pp.

Reeves' book is straight autobiography, covering his study as a singer, his debut in *Guy Mannering* in 1839, and his work at Drury Lane Theatre under Macready's management. Of particular interest here is Reeves' lengthy description of his training in Italy.

341a. *My Jubilee or Fifty Years of Artistic Life* by J.

Sims Reeves with Six Plates and a Preface by Thomas Ward. London: The London Music Publishing Co., and Simpkin, Marshall and Co. and Hamilton Adams and Co., 1889. 280 pp.

Reynolds, Frederick, 1764-1841.

342. *The Life and Times of Frederick Reynolds* written by himself. London: Henry Colburn, 1826. Two Volumes.

Reynolds' memoirs are wholly of the eighteenth-century theatre. He wrote his eighth and ninth comedies at the turn of the nineteenth century, having established himself as a writer of both plays and musical dramas at Drury Lane and Covent Garden Theatres.

342a. *The Life and Times of Frederick Reynolds* . . . Philadelphia. H. C. Cary and Lea, 1826. Two Volumes.

342b. *The Life and Times of Frederick Reynolds* . . . 2nd Ed. London: Henry Colburn, 1827. Two Volumes in One.

342c. *The Life and Times of Frederick Reynolds.* New York: Benjamin Blom, 1969. Two Volumes in One.

Reynolds, Harry, n.d.

343. *Minstrel Memories; The Story of Burnt Cork Minstrelsy in Great Britain from 1836 to 1927* by Harry Reynolds. London: A. Rivers Co., 1928. 255 pp.

This book is primarily a history of ministrelsy. However, the last sections are Reynold's memoirs of being the creator of "Harry Reynold's Minstrels." The many photographs and programs he includes provide a comprehensive record of nineteenth-century minstrel life.

Rhys, Charles Horton, 1824-1876.

344. *A Theatrical Trip for a Wager! Through Canada and the United States* by Captain Charles Horton Rhys ("Morton Price"). London: Printed for the author by Charles Dudley, 1861. 140 pp.

On a bet, Rhys, an author and amateur actor, toured America in 1859 in an attempt to earn 500 pounds by acting. In a year he returned to England, broke, having lost the bet. The book is more of a travelogue than a theatre memoir. To his comments on travel in the United States and Canada, he adds copies of programs and a hotel menu.

Rice, Edward LeRoy, 1871-

345. *Monarches of Minstrelsey, From "Daddy" Rice to Date* by Edward LeRoy Rice. New York: Kenny Publishing Co., 1911. 366 pp.

The first four pages of Rice's book are autobiographical. The rest is his first-hand recollection of minstrel performers. Of particular interest are sketches of Daddy Rice, Billy Birch and Lew Dockstadler.

Ristori, Adelaide, 1822-1906.

346. *Memoirs and Artistic Studies of Adelaide Ristori.* Rendered into English by G. Mantellini; With Biographical Appendix by L. D. Ventura; Illustrated from Photographs and Engravings. London: W. H. Allen and Co., 1888. 263 pp.

Adelaide Ristori was brought on stage as a three-month-old infant, was an actress at ten years old and leading lady in her native Italy at nineteen years old. She became famous first in France after her meeting with Dumas and Rachel. In her memoir, which includes comments on her tours of Europe and North and South America, she gives attention to the development of her roles as Mary Stuart, Medea, Phaedra, Lady MacBeth and Queen Elizabeth. Few such meticulous studies of particular roles emerge in other memoirs. She considers motivation, stage business, attitude and the costuming of each scene.

346a. *Adelaide Ristori. Studies and Memoirs. An Autobiography.* Boston: Robert Brothers, 1888. 297 pp.

346b. *Memoirs and Artistic Studies.* New York: Doubleday, Page and Co., 1907. 263 pp.

Ritchie, Mrs. Anna Cora. See Mowatt, Anna Cora.

Roberts, Arthur, 1852-1933.

347. *The Adventures of Arthur Roberts by Rail, Road, and River* told by Himself and Chronicled by Richard Morton. Bristol: J. W. Arrowsmith and London: Simpkin, Marshall, Hamilton, Kent and Co., 1895. 198 pp.

Roberts began penny readings at thirteen, then began singing in concert halls, and went on tour as a singer and comic. He worked in the early music halls in London, where he became particularly noted as a pantomime artist. At one time he managed a company and toured as its star.

348. *Fifty Years of Spoof* by Arthur Roberts. London: J. Lane, 1927. 255 pp.

Roberts enlarges on his earlier memoirs of a music hall career as pantomimist, singer and comic. Included are descriptions of the very early days of London's music halls before they earned the respect of the theatre-going public.

Robertson, Walford Graham, 1867-1948.

349. *Time Was: The Reminiscences of W. Graham Robertson*: With a Foreword by Sir Johnstone Forbes-Robertson. London: Hamish Hamilton, 1931. 343 pp.

Robertson stresses his primary career as a painter and his secondary careers as stage designer, costumer and dramatist. His special interest in these memoirs is Sarah Bernhardt, but he also sketches Ellen Terry, Nellie Farren, Henry Irving, Whistler, Sargent and other painters and actors of his day.

349a. *Life was Worth Living; the Reminiscences of W. Graham Robertson* . . . New York: Harpers, 1931. 343 pp.

This is the American edition of *Time Was*.

349b. *Time Was* . . . London: Hamish Hamilton, 1933. 343 pp.

349c. *Time Was* . . . London: Hamish Hamilton, 1945. 343 pp.

Robey, George, 1869-1954.

350. *Looking Back on Life* by George Robey with an Introduction, "Mr. Robey, Auctioneer," by Sir James Barrie, Bart., London: Constable and Co., 1933. 318 pp.

Although Robey started out to be an engineer like his father, his hobby of giving after dinner concerts led him to a career in England's music halls, during which he often played several halls in one night. Although he moved into England's patent theatres in the twentieth century, his nineteenth-century years were spent in association with Dan Leno, Marie Lloyd, Vesta Tilley, Albert Chevalier and other music hall entertainers.

350a. *Looking Back on Life* . . . London: Constable and Co., 1934. 318 pp.

351. *My Life Up Till Now. A Naughtibiography* Illustrated by George Robey. London: Greening and Co., 1908. 128 pp.

Robey's early memoirs are entirely of his early break into show business and his climb to success in what were then considered to be London's naughty music halls.

351a. *My Life Up Till Now* . . . London: Greening and Co., 1909. 128 pp.

Robins, Elizabeth, 1862/65-1952.

352. *Both Sides of the Curtain* by Elizabeth Robins. London and Toronto: W. Heinemann, 1940. 331 pp.

By 1888 Robins had played in the companies of Edwin Booth and James O'Neill. Most of this memoir is about her emergence on the London stage in 1889 and her introduction to Ibsen's plays. Robins, who was also very prolific as a writer, is informative about the ways in which parts were assigned to actors, the contacts that had to be cultivated to pursue parts in England, and the help she received from Oscar Wilde in what was a difficult task: securing a position in a good English company even though she was an American.

Robinson, Josephine. See Mott, Josephine.

Rogers, Clara Kathleen, 1844-1931.

353. *Memories of a Musical Career* by Clara Kathleen Rogers. Boston: Little, Brown Co., 1919. 503 pp.

Clara Rogers' *Memories* begin with her childhood and end with her marriage in 1878. Particularly useful here are descriptions of student life at the Leipzig Conservatory of Music in Berlin and the social and professional life of opera stars, who seemingly were more welcome in polite society than were actors.

353a. *Memories of a Musical Career* . . . Norwood, Mass.: Privately Printed by the Plimpton Press, 1932. 503 pp.

354. *The Story of Two Lives. Home, Friends, and Travel.* Norwood, Massachusetts: Privately printed at the Plimpton Press, 1932. 348 pp.

Rogers' second memoir begins where the first stopped, with her marriage to a Boston lawyer. While the first stresses her operatic training and career, the second stresses prominent characters, and the high society of Boston. The picture she paints of the comfortable life in the 1880s and 90s in America is especially interesting.

Ross, Frederick G., 1858-1942.

355. *The Actor From Point Arena.* Excerpts Taken From "Memories of an Old Theatrical Man" by Frederick G. Ross. Edited With a Commentary by Travis Bogard. Berkeley: The Friends of the Bancroft Library, 1977. 38 pp.

This volume is the edited version of a lengthy, unpublished typescript by Ross. Ross debuted in 1879 as a super in a San Francisco theatre. The book chronicles his experiences at the California Theatre and the Baldwin Theatre stock company, where he played with James O'Neill, Tom Keane, and Frank Mayo. Ross remained a journeyman professional who never rose above supporting roles.

Rosslyn, James Francis, 1869-1939.

356. *My Gamble With Life* by the Earl of Rosslyn. London: Cassell, 1928. 309 pp.

Rosslyn has high praise for the amateur theatricals in which he began acting in 1894. After leaving bankruptcy court in 1897, he decided to go on the professional stage, signing a contract under the pseudonym of James Erskine. There is in his autobiography a brief description of his seven years on the stage and cast lists of the plays in which he appeared.

356a. *My Gamble With Life*. New York: J. H. Sears and Co., 1928. 320 pp.

Russell, Henry, 1812-1899/1900.

357. *Cheer! Boys, Cheer! Memories of Men and Music* by Henry Russell. London: J. Macqueen, 1895. 276 pp.

Russell made his debut in an operatic production as a child of eight. He writes of opera and musical theatre, but particularly of non-theatrical matters impressed upon him on a tour to the United States, where he carefully observed American Indians, Blacks, and rural folk.

Russell, Henry, 1871-1937.

358. *The Passing Show*. Boston: Little, Brown and Co., 1926. 296 pp.

This English impresario caught the attention of Nellie Melba and others when he was a young man, launching a career that began in London in the 1890s. At the turn of the century, shortly after his debut, Russell moved to the United States. Although most of his career is in the twentieth century, he does write about the city of London at the end of the nineteenth century and the theatrical conflict between the syndicate and the Schuberts that occurred just after his arrival in the U.S.

358a. *The Passing Show*. London: Thornton Butterworth Co., 1926. 295 pp.

Ryan, Kate, 1857-1922.

359. *Old Boston Museum Days* by Kate Ryan. Boston: Little, Brown and Co., 1915. 264 pp.

Ryan, a member of the old Boston Museum from 1872 to 1893, portrays individual actors who appeared there. She makes a study of the stock company--its members on and off stage. That Ryan is able to study one company over a period of many years is unusual in theatre memoirs.

359a. *Old Boston Museum Days* by Kate Ryan. St. Clair Shores, Michigan: Scholarly Press, 1971. 264 pp.

Ryley, Samuel William, 1759-1837.

360. *The Itinerant, or Memoirs of an Actor* by S. W. Ryley. Volume 1. London: Taylor and Hessey, 1808. Volumes Two and Three. London: Sherwood, Neely Jones, 1809; Volume Four. London: Sherwood, Neely and Jones, 1816. Volumes Five and Six. London: Sherwood, Nelly and Jones, 1817. Volumes Seven, Eight and Nine. London: Sherwood and Co.; Edinburgh: Constable Co.; Glasgow: Griffin Co., 1827. Nine Volumes.

The ninth and last volume of Ryley's *Autobiography* includes some nineteenth-century materials, specifically a long section on Robert Bradbury, a clown who was accepted in polite society. Fashions, manners, courtship and society in general are delineated here.

360a. *The Itinerant . . .* Philadelphia: Printed and Sold by J. and A. Y. Humphreys "Cange-wald," corner of Second and Walnut streets, 1810. Two Volumes.

360b. *The Itinerant . . .* New York: Inskeep and Bradford, 1810. Two Volumes.

360c. *The Adventures of an Actor, or Life of a Strolling Player*. London: W. Dugdale, 18--. Two Volumes.

This is an abridged edition of *The Itinerant.*

360d. *The Itinerant . . .* Philadelphia: Humphreys, 1811. Two Volumes.

360e. *The Itinerant . . .* Philadelphia: M. Carey and Son, 1817. Two Volumes.

360f. *The Adventures of an Actor, or, Life of a Strolling Player*. New Abridged Edition. Loewenberg, 1860. Two Volumes.

S

Sala, George Augustus, 1828-1895.

361. *Life and Adventures of George Augustus Sala* Written by Himself. London: Cassell, 1895. Two Volumes.

As a child Sala was well acquainted with musicians and actors whom his mother, a singer, entertained in their home. He knew Bellini, Malibran and Oscar Wilde. At age fifteen he worked at a variety of backstage jobs at the Princess' Theatre. Though he wrote a few plays, he is primarily known as a journalist, critic, and war correspondent. Much of his information is non-theatrical: the death of the Tsar, Spanish royalty, Garibaldi, the Prince of Wales. Some of his material is on the theatre that he knew intimately. One entire chapter is devoted to greenrooms.

Salvini, Tommaso, 1829-1916.

362. *Leaves From the Autobiography of Tommaso Salvini.* New York: Century Press, 1893. 240 pp.

Salvini's first appearance on stage was at fourteen years old with an Italian company in which his father was leading man. At fifteen he was orphaned, and he had to make his own way. For a time he fought with Garibaldi's forces, but returned to the stage, having learned many techniques of survival from the famous managers with whom he had worked in his youth, particularly Modena and Ristori. These memoirs, more than most others, give attention to acting as a craft. He comments on voice control, facial expression, and physical training, and compares the acting styles of different nationalities. He also has professional critiques of his fellow actors: Bernhardt, Ristori, Rachel, Edwin Booth and Henry Irving.

362a. *Leaves From the Autobiography* . . . New York: Benjamin Blom, 1971. 240 pp.

Sanger, George, 1825/26-1911.

363. *Seventy Years a Showman by "Lord" George Sanger; My Life and Adventures in Camp and Caravan The World Over.* London: G. A. Pearson, 1908. 128 pp.

Sanger's entire world was the circus. His father was an itinerant showman who carried a "peep shop box" of historical events on his back. Sanger began his own show while still in his teens. His caravans brought him into contact with grave robbers, lynchings, Chartist riots and a small pox epidemic. He was engaged in many areas of entertainment, from magic acts to animal training and, incidentally, play production, for circuses often included the performance of a play. His success brought him the proprietorship of Astley's where he remained for twenty-two years.

363a. *Seventy Years a Showman* . . . London: J. M. Dent and Sons, 1926. 287 pp.

363b. *Seventy Years a Showman* . . . New York: E. P. Dutton and Co., 1926. 249 pp.

363c. *Seventy Years a Showman* . . . London: J. M. Dent and Co., 1927. 257 pp.

363d. *Seventy Years a Showman* . . . London: J. M. Dent and Co., 1935. 256 pp.

363e. *Seventy Years a Showman* . . . London: J. M. Dent and Co., 1938. 176 pp.

363f. *Seventy Years a Showman* . . . London: J. M. Dent and Co., 1952. 256 pp.

Santley, Charles, 1834-1922.

364. *Reminiscences of My Life* by Charles Santley. London: I. Pitman and Sons, 1909. 319 pp.

Santley was one of the foremost British baritones of his day. This memoir begins with his return to England in 1872. He writes not only of his operatic career, but of his relationship to the famous Kemble family and his journeys to various places throughout the world.

364a. *Reminiscences of My Life.* New York: Bretano's, 1909. 318 pp.

364b. *Reminiscences of My Life.* New York: Arno Press, 1977. 319 pp.

365. *Student and Singer. The Reminiscences of Charles Santley.* London: Edward Arnold, 1892. 327 pp.

Santley covers in some detail his early life and aspirations, his introduction to the theatre as an operatic singer, his study in Italy and subsequent professional career abroad and at home.

365a. *Student and Singer . . .* New York: Macmillan and Co., 1892. 358 pp.

365b. *Student and Singer.* New Edition. London: Edward Arnold, 1893. 358 pp.

Sartain, John, 1808-1897.

366. *The Reminiscences of a Very Old Man, 1808-1897.* By John Sartain. New York: D. Appleton, 1889. 297 pp.

At twelve years old John Sartain began work as a theatrical pyrotechnist, producing "steam, smoke and fire" at the Theatre Royal, Covent Garden. His two chapters on his association with Kemble and company include details about his particular craft and about backstage life in general.

366a. *The Reminiscences of a Very Old Man . . .* New York: D. Appleton, 1900. 297 pp.

366b. *The Reminiscences of a Very Old Man . . .* New York: D. Appleton, 1910. 297 pp.

366c. *The Reminiscences of a Very Old Man . . .* New York: Benjamin Blom, 1969. 297 pp.

Scott, Cyril, 1866-1946.

367. *My Years of Indiscretion* by Cyril Scott. London: Mills and Boon, 1924. 282 pp.

Scott was trained as a composer and pianist under Uzielli and while very young heard a symphony orchestra in Frankfurt perform his work. He writes not only of his own musical performances, but also of his knowledge of literary circles, particularly poets in Germany and England. Other interesting topics in his memoirs include spiritual philosophy, free love and Debussy.

Shaw, George Bernard, 1856-1950.

368. *An Autobiography 1856-1898 and 1898-1950.* New York: Weybright and Talley, 1969-70. Two Volumes.

In Volume One, covering the years 1856 through 1898, Shaw remembers his childhood in Dublin: the genteel poverty of his family in London during his young manhood, his introduction to Fabianism, his career as a literary, music and drama critic and the beginning of his years as a playwright. Also see the many collections of Shaw's letters.

368a. *An Autobiography 1856-1898 and 1898-1950.* New York: Weybright and Talley, 1969-70. Two Vols.

Shaw, Martin, 1875-1958.

369. *Up to Now* by Martin Shaw. London: H. Milford, 1929. 218 pp.

A child of a musical family, Shaw was taught to play the piano and organ before he could remember. After training as a musician at the Royal College of Music, he founded the Purcell Operatic Society in 1899 with Gordon Craig as stage director, producing "a new era in theatrical art." In further association with Craig and Craig's mother, Ellen Terry, Shaw began several experimental theatres which were artistic but not financial successes.

Sherwood, Robert Edmund, 1864-1946.

370. *Here We Are Again. Recollections of an Old Circus Clown* by Robert Edmund Sherwood. Indianapolis: Bobbs-Merrill Co., 1926. 292 pp.

Sherwood ran away to join the circus at nine years old as Dan Rice's apprentice in 1867. He gives a history of the circus in the United States as he saw it first-hand. Sherwood's memoirs are valuable as a record of how children were trained for the circus at this time and the extent to which the clergy antagonized the circus. He also illustrates that circus performers frequently joined stock companies in off-seasons. He, for example, enjoyed being cast as the grave-digger in *Hamlet*.

371. *Hold Yer Hosses! The Elephants are Coming.* New York: The Macmillan Co., 1932. 361 pp.

The first chapter of this book is a history of the circus. The second chapter is the beginning of Sherwood's own story. He writes of joining Dan Rice's circus when he was ten years old for a four-year apprenticeship as an acrobat. From 1875 to 1894 he worked as a clown and acrobat for Barnum. In the winter months, during off-season, he was an actor, playing occasionally at theatres of the stature of McVickers in Chicago. Most of his memories, however, are of the circus: Barnum, Forepaugh, Elbert Hubbard, curiosities and circus animals.

Simond, Ike, n.d.

372. *Old Slacks Reminiscences and Pocket History of the Colored Profession. From 1865 to 1891* by Ike Simond, Banjo Comique. Chicago: n.p., 1892. 33 pp.

Simond includes little information about himself, but describes, from first-hand observation, all the minstrel troupes and all the black performers he has come across in opera, drama, circuses and music houses.

372a. *Old Slacks* . . . Bowling Green, Ohio: Popular Press, 1974. 123 pp.

Sims, George R., 1847-1922.

373. *My Life; Sixty Years' Recollections of Bohemian London*. By George R. Sims. London: Eveleigh Nash Co., 1917. 351 pp.

Sims began his association with the theatre at age twenty-four as a drama critic for satirical journals such as *Punch* and *Fun*. In 1879 he saw produced his own play, *Crutch and Toothpick*. His special love was the literary burlesque and light comedy. He wrote *Blue Eyed Susan, The Merry Duchess*, and *The Lights O'London*. His struggles as a playwright and his many acquaintances in the theatre, especially Augustus Harris, Louis Diehl and Wilson Barrett, are his subjects.

Skinner, Otis, 1858-1942.

374. *Footlights and Spotlights; Recollections of My Life on the Stage* by Otis Skinner. New York: Blue Ribbon Books, 1913, 366 pp.

Skinner, who made his debut at the Philadelphia Museum in 1877, had the good fortune of acting with many of the great stars of the last two decades of the century in stock companies. In this memoir he covers three of those years with more than the usual skill, while commenting on styles of acting, the many different aspects of production, and the changes taking place in the theatre at that time.

374a. *Footlights and Spotlights* . . . New York: Blue Ribbon Books, 1924. 366 pp.

374b. *Footlights and Spotlights* . . . Indianapolis: The Bobbs-Merrill Co., 1924. 366 pp.

374c. *Footlights and Spotlights*. Westport, Conn.: Greenwood Press, 1972. 366 pp.

Smart, George Thomas, 1776-1867.

375. *Leaves From the Journal of Sir George Smart* by H. Bertram Cox and C.L.E. Cox. London, New York, Bombay and Calcutta: Longman, Green and Co., 1907. 355 pp.

Smart was, from 1813 to 1844, concert conductor of the Philharmonic Society. This is an edited version of journals and letters kept from childhood to 1845. They constitute records of expenses and receipts of various performances.

375a. *Leaves From the Journal of Sir George Smart.* New York: Da Capo Press, 1971. 355 pp.

Smedley, Constance, 1881-1941.

376. *Crusaders. The Reminiscences of Constance Smedley* (Mrs. Maxwell Armfield). London: Duckworth, 1929. 265 pp.

Constance Smedley, a dramatist and novelist, was introduced to the theatre in the 1890s when she began submitting her plays to managers and actors. Though her plays were never produced in the nineteenth century, her early efforts brought her recognition from Mrs. Patrick Campbell, Cyril Maude and Violet Vanbrugh, beginning a life-long relationship with the stage.

Smith, Harry Bache, 1860-1936.

377. *First Nights and First Editions* by Harry B. Smith. Boston: Little, Brown and Co., 1931. 325 pp.

Smith, who began writing musicals in 1884, wrote more than three hundred plays, including adaptations from the French and German. He collaborated with Victor Herbert on *Serenade*. His memoirs include anecdotes about music and theatre celebrities of his acquaintance at the turn of the twentieth century.

Smith, Solomon, 1801-1869.

378. *The Theatrical Apprenticeship and Four Anecdotal Recollections of Sol Smith . . . Comprising a Sketch of the First Seven Years of His Professional Life; Together With Some Sketches of Adventure in After Years.* Philadelphia: Carey and Hart, 1846. 215 pp.

Smith writes of his first seven years of theatre apprenticeship--being hopelessly stage struck, following touring shows, attempting in his poverty to teach and to run a printing office. His association with pioneer theatrical manager James H. Caldwell helped launch his own important company in what was then the southwest. Also included are anecdotes, chiefly involving townspeople along the tour with whom the actors had to associate, letters defending the stage to clergymen, and a portrait of himself from the *New World*.

378a. *The Theatrical Apprenticeship . . .* Philadelphia: Carey and Hart, 1851. 215 pp.

378b. *The Theatrical Apprenticeship . . .* Philadelphia: T. B. Peterson, 1854. 215 pp.

379. *The Theatrical Journey-Work and Anecdotical Recollections of Sol. Smith . . . Comprising a Sketch of the Second Seven Years of His Professional Life; Together with Sketches of Adventure in After Years; With a Portrait of the Author.* Philadelphia: T. B. Peterson, 1854. 254 pp.

> Sol Smith's *Journey-Work* is exceedingly valuable not only for its view of a primitive, growing theatre which often played in lofts and barns, but for its window on the frontier--the Indians, the rural south, its politics, manners, and religions. Detailed accounts of expenses, profits and improvised stages and theatres on the frontier are given. The work ends with several defenses of stage and actors, two written as replies to ministers who had attacked the stage.

380. *Theatrical Management in the West and South for Thirty Years Interspersed with Anecdotical Sketches*; Autobiographically Given by Sol. Smith. With Fifteen Illustrations and a Portrait of the Author. New York: Harper and Brothers, 1868. 275 pp.

> Much of the material and many of the illustrations from the apprenticeship and journey-work are repeated here. Added are several new defenses of the stage, a record of correspondence, transactions of a "Committee on Authors and Amateurs," and a committee to erect a statue of Shakespeare in Central Park.

380a. *Theatrical Management in the West and South . . .* American Culture Series 45: 6. Ann Arbor: University Microfilms, 1956. 275 pp.

380b. *Theatrical Management in the West and South . . .* New York: Benjamin Blom, 1968. 294 pp.

Soldene, Emily, 1840-1912.

381. *My Theatrical and Musical Recollections* by Emily Soldene with Seven Portraits. London: Downey and Co., 1897. 315 pp.

> Emily Soldene, a singer, appeared in opera and opera bouffe. Her first professional appearance was in *Il Trovatore* in 1865 at Drury Lane. She was afterward a regular starring performer at major theatres in the British Isles and made four tours of the United States. She recalls her career with a tone of nostalgia, commenting on people, places, theatres, costuming, staging and rehearsals.

381a. *My Theatrical and Musical Recollections . . .* 2nd Ed. London: Downey and Co., 1897. 315 pp.

381b. *My Theatrical and Musical Recollections . . .* New Ed. London: Downey and Co., 1898. 315 pp.

381c. *My Theatrical and Musical Recollections . . .* New Ed. London: T. S. Clarke, 1906. 315 pp.

Sothern, Edward Hugh, 1859-1933.

382. *Melancholy Tale of 'Me'; My Remembrances* by Edward H. Sothern. New York: Scribners, 1916. 409 pp.

> A goodly portion of Sothern's memoir is about his childhood as the son of an actor and his eccentric father who developed the role of Lord Dundreary. He also writes of an even more ecentric uncle, Hugh Stewart, who made an abortive attempt to rescue Chinese Gordon. The last of the book is about his own first steps as an actor and his management of the Lyceum in New York.

382a. *My Remembrances; The Melancholy Tale of 'Me'* by Edward H. Sothern. London and New York: Cassell and Co., 1917. 409 pp.

Stirling, Edward, 1809/11-1894.

383. *Old Drury Lane. Fifty Years' Recollections of Author, Actor, and Manager* by Edward Stirling. London: Chatto and Windus, 1881. Two Volumes.

> Stirling toured the provinces of England for many years as an actor before going to Drury Lane as manager. He includes a survey of London managers during his time at Drury Lane, a history of Drury Lane, and sketches of actors who appeared at Drury Lane.

Stoddart, James Henry, 1827-1907.

384. *Recollections of a Player* by J. H. Stoddart. New York: The Century Co., 1902. 225 pp.

> Although born in England, Stoddard came to the United States in 1854 to remain for the rest of his life. His career spans half a century of American theatre. His subjects are the James W. Wallack Company, Laura Keene's Varieties, his tours of the U.S. and Canada, the Mobile Theatre of Pre-Civil War days and his association with A. M. Palmer at the Union Square and Madison Square Theatres.

Stoker, Bram

385. *Personal Reminiscences of Henry Irving* by Bram Stoker. London: William Heinemann, 1906. Two Volumes.

Stoker's business association with Irving began in 1878 soon after which he took charge of Irving's business affairs and served as acting manager of his company. Despite the title, this is not a life of Irving, but a chronicle of personal associations. He comments on acting, plays, playwrights, theatre personnel, stage business, rehearsals, tours, and, in particular, the methods of Henry Irving.

Stone, Fred Andrew, 1873-1959.

386. *Rolling Stone* by Fred Stone. New York and London: Whittlesey House Publications and McGraw Hill, 1945. 246 pp.

As a boy Fred Stone was a tight-rope walker with a circus, a position he gave up as a young man in order to do a minstrel act in opera houses and dime museums. He writes of these entertainments as they flourished in the far west in the 1880s and 1890s. In the twentieth century, he became an actor and created his most famous role, the straw man in the Wizard of Oz.

Sumbel, Mary. See Wells, Mary.

Swears, Herbert, 1869-1946.

387. *When All's Said and Done*. London: Geoffrey Bliss, 1937. 304 pp.

Herbert Swears writes of his decision to leave his position with the Bank of England to become an actor and, eventually, a playwright. The first 200 pages of his memoir describe his nineteenth-century associations with such notables as Charles Brookfield, Forbes-Robertson, Charles Hawtrey, Henry Irving and H. B. Tree.

T

Taylor, Joe, 1834-

388. *Joe Taylor, Barnstormer, His Travels, Troubles and Triumphs, During Fifty Years in Footlight Flashes* by Justus Hurd Taylor; With Illustrations by Ripley. New York: William R. Jenkins Co., 1913. 248 pp.

In his fifty years of touring Taylor saw and recorded gun fights, duels, rowdy audiences, and travel on foot, by wagon and by sailing ship. He performed under the most primitive conditions imaginable in western mining towns. As gambler, fighter and pool hustler, he went from town to town, from country to country, including Australia, Hawaii, and the British Isles. In the United States he saw old performers freezing to death in the Rocky Mountains, and he played with Lotta Crabtree in her first black-face role. In Shanghai, the play he acted in was performed in a billiard hall; in China he met "Chinese" Gordon.

Taylor, John, 1811-

389. *Autobiography of a Lancashire Lawyer, Being the Life and Recollections of John Taylor, Attorney-at Law, and First Coroner of the Borough of Bolton, With Notice of Many Persons and Things Met With During a Life of Seventy-two Years Lived in and about Bolton.* Ed. James Glegg. Bolton: The Daily Chronicle Office; Manchester: Tubbs, Brook, and Chrystal, 1883. 361 pp.

Taylor describes his training for the stage in the early nineteenth century. For a time he combined his law career with acting, performing with such notables as Sam Phelps, the Vandenhoffs, and Mrs. Stirling. In 1842, however, he gave up the stage altogether, even to the extent of giving away his theatre library and wardrobe because he decided that his association with the stage was "detrimental to my position in society." The book contains a few pages that are useful as a reflection of the social status of the stage in the first half of the century.

Terriss, Ellaline, 1871-1971.

390. *Ellaline Terriss* by Herself and With Others. London: Cassell, 1928. 299 pp.

The first of Ellaline Terriss' two books of memoirs was written while she was still performing on stage. Her subjects are her professional success and her personal life as wife of actor Seymour Hicks.

391. *Just a Little Bit of String*. With a Foreword by Beverly Nichols. Illustratred. London: Hutchinson, 1955.

Ellaline Terriss, daughter of William Terriss, wife of Seymour Hicks and a prominent actress in her own right, recorded these memoirs when she was eighty years old. Her subjects are her marriage to Seymour Hicks, the company of Charles Wyndham, with whom she played for many seasons, and the characters she played, the most famous being *Bluebell in Faeryland*, written by Walter Slaughter and her husband, Seymour Hicks.

Terry, Ellen, 1847-1928.

392. *The Story of My Life* by Ellen Terry. London: Hutchinson and Co., 1908. 381 pp.

Ellen Terry, the child of actors, made her debut at the age of eight on the stage with Charles Kean in *The Winter's Tale*. She continued to act until her marriage when she was sixteen to G. F. Watts. She writes of meeting Disraeli, Gladstone and Tennyson at this time. After the dissolution of her marriage to Watts, she returned to the stage but married again, and again left the stage, this time for six years. She was hired by the Bancrofts when she began practicing her profession again, but a few seasons later she left their company to enter into one of the most famous partnerships in stage history: she went to the Lyceum with Henry Irving. Terry has special chapters on the relationship of actor and playwright; her particular example of a writer for the stage is Charles Reade. The last half of her memoirs is a history of the Lyceum's productions and management. (Also see her correspondence with Bernard Shaw.)

392a. *The Story of My Life*. New York: The McClure Co., 1908. 407 pp.

392b. *The Story of My Life . . .* New York: Page and Co., 1909. 407 pp.

392c. *The Story of My Life . . .* 2nd Ed. London: Hutchinson and Co., 1920. 381 pp.

392d. *The Story of My Life . . .* London: Hutchinson and Co., 1922. 381 pp.

392e. *Ellen Terry's Memoirs.* Preface Notes and Additional Biographical Chapters by Edith Craig and Christopher St. John. New York: Putnam's Sons, 1932. 367 pp.

This is a reprint of *The Story of My Life* with biographical material from 1906 to 1928 added.

392f. *Ellen Terry's Memoirs . . .* London: V. Gollancz, 1933. 359 pp.

392g. *Ellen Terry's Memoirs.* New York: Benjamin Blom, 1969. 367 pp.

392h. *Ellen Terry's Memoirs.* Westport, Connecticut: Greenwood Press, 1970. 367 pp.

Thomas, Augustus, 1957-1934.

393. *The Print of My Remembrance* by Augustus Thomas . . . Illustrated With Photographs and Numerous Drawings by the Author. New York: Charles Scribner's Sons, 1922. 477 pp.

A. M. Palmer hired this actor-playwright to take the place of Dion Boucicault at the Madison Square theatre. Thomas concentrates on the great growth and changes occurring in the theatre at that time: the development of new character types encouraged by immigration, the replacement of the old run-and-groove sets by boxed scenes, and the birth of the combination system. Although his lack of chronology often makes his story difficult to follow, his is one of the most vivid accounts of theatrical and non-theatrical life in the United States in the 1880s. He writes of every-day life in New York City and on the Arizona frontier, of politics in the country, and of the special life of actors in the city.

Thomson, Christopher Birdwood, 1799-

394. *Autobiography of an Artisan* by Christopher Thomson. London: J. Chapman; Nottingham: J. Shaw and Sons, 1847. 408 pp.

Chapter Seven of his autobiography is devoted to theatrical matters. Thomson enlarges on his career as a strolling player in fit-ups and circuses and touring rustic regions where Shakespeare was unknown. The technical aspects of production are stressed. He also gives a good picture of the suffering of the poor actor who has to travel with a family.

Thurston, Howard, 1869-1936.

395. *My Life of Magic* by Howard Thurston. Philadelphia: Dorrance and Co., 1929. 273 pp.

Thurston was an accomplished writer and magician who left the Ohio farm in 1892 at age twenty-two to join the circus as a magician. He writes of his struggles upon the failure of the circus and his development of an independent act which was often a part of variety shows.

Tilley, Vesta, 1864-1952.

396. *Recollections of Vesta Tilley* by Lady DeFrece; With a Foreword by Sir Oswald Stoll, and an Appreciation by Sir Alfred Butt, Bart., With 44 Illustrations. London: Hutchinson, 1934.

Vesta Tilley went on stage at four years old and continued performing, chiefly in juvenile male roles, until adulthood. Although she is primarily remembered for her work in London's music halls (the principle subject of her recollections), she also filled engagements at Drury Lane Theatre.

Tillman, Frances Nelson, n.d.

397. *A Little Girl Goes Barnstorming* by Frances Nelson Tillman. Baltimore: Barton-Gillet Co., 1939. 35 pp.

No dates are available on the life of Frances Tillman, probably because she left her profession as soon as she grew up. She did, however, write an engaging memoir of her impressions as a child in what appears to be the 1880s and 90s, traveling with her family's troupe through the midwest and far west. She records valuable impressions of mining camps with their improvised theatres and sets, and their flash pans and lime lights.

Toole, John Lawrence, 1830-1906.

398. *Reminiscences of J. L. Toole*; Related by Himself and Chronicled by Joseph Hatton . . . Illustrated by Alfred Bryan and W. H. Margetson. London: Hurst and Blackett, 1889. Two Volumes.

A specialist in burlesque, Toole's first successes were in Dublin and Edinburgh, but he moved on to become an institution in London's Lyceum, where he appeared with the Bancrofts and Henry Irving and became a particular favorite of Charles Dickens. In these memoirs, which are often told in third person, one finds random anecdotes about Paul Bedford, Edmund Yates, E. H. Sothern and others. Volume Two includes a defense of the stage.

398a. *Reminiscences . . .* 3rd Ed. London: Hurst and Blackett, 1889. 447 pp.

398b. *Reminiscences . . .* An Abridged Version. London: G. Routledge and Sons, 1892. 281 pp.

Tree, Ellen. See Kean, Charles John and Tree, Ellen.

Truax, Sarah, 1877-

399. *A Woman of Parts; Memories of a Life on Stage.* New York: Longmans, Green, 1949. 247 pp.

Truax was educated at the Chicago Conservatory of Music and Dramatic Art where she made her first appearances. For three years she was engaged in a company whose star was Otis Skinner, and by the twentieth century she had secured a position with the Shuberts. Many aspects of production, little known to the general public, are included here: the particular machinery and equipment taken on tour by the company, the use made of stoves, wet plaster, borders, entrance numbers, wigs, and padding. She also comments briefly on the "cribs" in New Orleans, which would later be notorious as part of Storyville.

Turnour, Jules, 1876-1931.

400. *Autobiography of a Clown* as told to Isaac Marcosson; Illustrated by Mary Gardner. New York: Moffat, Yard and Co., 1910. 102 pp.

Turnour was born in a circus wagon of English circus performers. As a young boy he was apprenticed to acrobats and became a "human baseball" for other acrobats to toss or twirl. At sixteen many accidents had put an end to his future as an acrobat so he turned to clowning and made his way to the United States. This is a good first-hand history of circus life in the United States: the beginning of tent shows, the relationship of circus acts to the menagerie and "monster shows," and the store of circus clown tricks.

400a. *Autobiography of a Clown . . .* New York: Dodd, 1931. 98 pp.

Tyler, George C., 1867-1946.

401. *Whatever Goes Up. The Hazardous Fortunes of a Natural Born Gambler* by George C. Tyler in Collaboration with J. C. Furnas; With a Word of Introduction by Booth Tarkington. Indianapolis: The Bobbs-Merrill Co., 1934. 317 pp.

Tyler was manager, producer and director who at twelve years old jumped a freight to explore Florida and the west. When he returned, his father, to keep him at home, set him up as the manager of his hometown opera house in Ohio. Tyler broke into New York show business as a theatre reporter and was for five years an advance agent. By the end of the century he was a highly successful manager of Liebner and Co., an enterprise which lasted until World War I.

V

Vanbrugh, Irene, 1872-1949.

402. *To Tell My Story*. New York and London: Hutchinson and Co., 1949. 217 pp.

Like her older sister Violet, Irene got her first break in Sarah Thorne's stock company. Her first London engagement was made possible through the intervention of Lewis Carroll, a family friend. In the course of her career she acted in James M. Barrie's first play, went to Australia with the company of J. L. Toole, mad friends with Oscar Wilde and married Dion Buicicault.

Vanbrugh, Violet, 1867-1942.

403. *Dare to Be Wise* by Violet Vanbrugh. London: Hodder and Stoughton Co., 1925. 160 pp.

Violet Vanbrugh describes the difficulty of breaking into the theatre in the 1880s in London. For a time while she was seeking work, Ellen Terry took her to live in her house. After much travail she found an engagement in a fit-up, but eventually was offered parts in the companies of J. L. Toole, the Kendals, Henry Irving, and Augustin Daly. Her description of rehearsals at the Lyceum is one of the best. The last third of the book is advice to the aspiring actress, stressing the value of good training, a reputation for being responsible, and the cultivation of excellent health. She also is frank about the difficulties facing an actress who also wants a husband and children. She was married to Arthur Bourchier.

Vandenhoff, George, 1913-1885.

404. *Dramatic Reminiscences; or, Actors and Actresses in England and America* by George Vandenhoff. Ed. With a Preface by Henry Seymour Carleton. London: Thomas W. Cooper and Co., and John Camden Hotten, 1860. 318 pp.

George Vandenhoff, son of actor John M. Vandenhoff, was first employed in Madame Vestris' Covent Garden Theatre. The directions he gives to aspiring actors includes a description of the backstage at Covent Garden's where company members had green rooms segregated by position in the theatre. He outlines the functions of each member of the production staff, including the call boy and dresser and describes the ceremony of distributing parts. He also indicates the effective way to study a part. His training of Catherine Sinclair and what he considered to be her shabby treatment of him occupy some of his attention. Vandenhoff also describes briefly a subject of which most visitors to New Orleans seemed unaware--the Quadroon Balls.

404a. *Leaves From An Actor's Notebook, With Reminiscences and Chitchat of the Green Room and the Stage, in England and America* by George Vandenhoff. New York: D. Appleton and Co., 1860. 347 pp.

To this American edition of *Dramatic Reminiscences,* Vandenhoff adds an expression of disenchantment with the stage similar to that expressed by Fanny Kemble and Macready. He decries the low state to which the theatre and public taste have sunk.

404b. *An Actor's Notebook: or, the Green-room and Stage.* Another ed. London: John Camden Hotten, 1865. 318 pp.

404c. *Leaves From an Actor's Notebook . . .* American Culture Series. Ann Arbor: University Microfilms, 1962. 347 pp.

Vernon-Harcourt, Frederick C., 1845-

405. *From Stage to Cross; The Record of a Rolling Stone* by F. C. Vernon-Harcourt. London: S. W. Partridge and Co., 1901. 312 pp.

Vernon-Harcourt, a soldier of fortune, writes memoirs which embrace many adventures in land and sea battles. His stage career was sandwiched between his participation in the Civil War and the Boer War. His is an unusual story of being a runaway among tramps, knowing the severe cruelties of a life at sea, witnessing Union officers torturing their own soldiers as punishment for minor offenses, and being himself imprisoned by Confederates as a spy. He considers his brief stage career his chief folly. He left the stage to become a speaker for the Liberal Party. After much wild carousing he gave up whiskey, was converted and became an evangelist.

W~Y

Wade, George Edward. See Robey, George.

Walker, Thomas, 1850-1934.

406. *From Sawdust to Windsor Castle* by "Whimsical Walker," London: Stanley Paul and Co., 1922. 247 pp.

At age twenty-three in 1875 Whimsical Walker ran away from home to join the circus. He rapidly rose to the best circuses in England and America as a clown. After an engagement at Astley's, he toured in the United States with Barnum and Bailey. He writes of circus management, animal training and, as the title suggests, his command performances.

Wallack, John Lester, 1819/20-1888.

407. *Memories of Fifty Years* With an Introduction by Laurence Hutton. New York: Charles Scribners Sons, 1889. 232 pp.

Wallack gives considerable attention to the great actors who strongly influenced his life: G. V. Brooke, Charles Mathews, William Mitchell, Macready and his own father. He also discursively relates his own career in anecdotal fashion: the time when John Brougham played *Pocahontas* without the leading lady; the time when the feud between Macready and Forrest erupted in the Astor Place Riot; the time when Laura Keene deserted his father's company just seconds before the curtain was to go up, and the time E. A. Sothern tried to refuse the part of Lord Dundreary before turning it into a legendary role. Wallack also looks at acting as a craft, commenting on various methods of study, including his own.

407a. *Memories of Fifty Years* . . . London: S. Low, Marston, Searle and Revington, 1889. 232 pp.

407b. *Memories of Fifty Years . . .* New York: Benjamin Blom, 1969. 232 pp.

Wallett, William Frederick, 1808-1892.

408. *The Public Life of W. F. Wallett, The Queen's Jester: An Autobiography of Forty Years' Professional Experience and Travels in the United Kingdom, the United States of America (Including California), Canada, South America, Mexico, the West Indies, Etc.* Ed. John Luntley. London and Derby: Benrose and Sons; London: Thomas Hailes Lacy; Edinburgh: John Menzies, 1870. 188 pp.

> Wallett, a scene painter, manager and clown, began his career by touring in small stock companies, booths, and circuses. When the circus was called to Windsor Castle, he had the opportunity of performing for Queen Victoria. After several years as a clown at Astly's, he formed his own circus and made a tour of America, where he encountered dangerous thieves and murderers on the frontier. The most interesting portion in the work is his description of the materials and machinery used by the primitive booths he worked in as a child.

408a. *The Public Life . . .* 2nd Ed. London: Thomas Hailes Lacy and others, . 188 pp.

408b. *The Public Life . . .* 3rd Ed. London: Thomas Hailes Lacy and others, . 188 pp.

Ward, Genevieve, 1838-1922.

409. *Both Sides of the Curtain* by Genevieve Ward and Richard Whiting: With a Colour Frontpiece and Sixteen Other Places. London and New York: Cassell and Co., 1918. 291 pp.

> Ward was an American opera singer who made her debut at La Scala in 1857 when she was twenty years old. After six years, she lost her voice and went on stage as an actress, touring America, Australia, Hawaii and South Africa. Her third career as a drama coach may explain her inclusion of material on methods of training actors and singers and discussions of the old and new schools of acting. She also compares opera of different nationalities and judges a variety of singers.

Warde, Frederick B., 1851-1935.

410. *Fifty Years of Make-Believe* by Frederick Warde. New York: The International Press Syndicate, 1920. 310 pp.

> Although Warde's career began in England, he moved to America around 1867 and began an association with Booth's Theatre that would last for three years. He toured with Booth, McCullough and Maurice Barrymore.

Warde makes good use of detail in describing the English fit-ups of his early days and the Lyceum Theatre at Sunderland. His account is made lively with vignettes and anecdotes, a few about amusing stage accidents.

410a. *Fifty Years of Make-Believe . . .* Los Angeles: Times Mirror Press, 1923. 314 pp.

Warren, Lavinia, 1841-1919.

411. *The Autobiography of Mrs. Tom Thumb (Some of My Life Experiences)* by Countess M. Lavinia Magri Formerly Mrs. General Tom Thumb. With the Assistance of Sylvester Bleeker. Ed. and Introduced by A. Saxon Hamden, Conn.: Archon Books, 1979. 199 pp.

Lavinia Warren, a "little person," was displayed by her cousin on a floating museum of curiosities where she was discovered by Barnum. Later she was married to "General Tom Thumb." After their wedding, one of the most elaborate functions of the decade, Barnum sponsored their world tour of singing, dancing and acting. Warren describes the old river boats, curiosities and minstrel shows, as well as her wedding and meeting with royalty from several countries on her tours.

Watkins, Harry, 1825-1894.

412. *One Man in His Time. The Adventure of H. Watkins Strolling Player, 1845-1863. From his Journal* by Maud and Otis Skinner. Philadelphia: University of Pennsylvania Press; London: H. Milford, Oxford University Press, 1938. 258 pp.

Skinner edits Harry Watkin's fragmentary journal, a study in the life of a player who appeared in Boston, Philadelphia, New York, New Orleans and in the rural areas of Ohio, Louisiana and Texas, often following the United States Army, which held a particular attraction for him. Watkins, perhaps because he was writing for himself, is more candid than any writer for the public would dare to be. He presents the seedier, seamier side of touring life--not only the poverty and physical harshness of the profession, but the violence, murder, thievery, desertion, and cheating--all among the actors and managers with whom he toured. The marriage that he made and rejected almost immediately, the child that was born to him and his wife in a hotel room on tour--these are matters that bring a harsh reality to the record Watkins left. Although he admitted being a very heavy drinker, he made a specialty of the temperance play, *The Drunkard*, a production that supposedly led scores of winos to take the pledge. His account of the Astor Place Riot is also valuable because he was in the street in front of the theatre when the shooting occurred. He writes of many minor and largely forgotten actors like himself and of Macready, Forrest, and Edwin Booth.

Wells, Mary, 1781-1826.

413. *Memoirs of the Life of Mrs. Sumbel, late Wells; of the Theatre-Royal, Drury-Lane, and Haymarket.* Written by Herself. Including her Correspondence With Major Topham, Mr. Reynolds the Dramatist, Etc., Etc., Etc. London: C. Chapple, 1811. Three Vols.

Although Mary Wells had worked as an actress at London's leading patent theatres and even speaks of an impending agreement to appear with Stephen Kemble, the turn of the nineteenth century found her fortunes going steadily downward. As a divorcee with two children, she came to be a poverty-striken itinerant, traveling from place to place only to be turned away from inns and refused food for herself and her children. A second marriage proves even worse than the first as her husband, an Arabian aristocrat, first tries to sell her, then imprisons her and finally deserts her. Her memoirs end with further misfortunes as her daughters are taken from her and then refuse to see her.

413a. *Memoirs* . . . Edgerley and Co., 1830.

Wemyss, Francis Courtney, 1797-1859.

414. *Twenty-Six Years of the Life of an Actor and Manager.* New York: Burgess, Stringer and Co., 1847. 324 pp.

Wemyss began his career by touring through Scotland and northern England. In 1822 he went to America to join the company of Warren and Wood. At a time when only the English were believed capable of high quality acting, Wemyss returned to England and brought a boat-load of actors back to America to stock American companies. Wemyss writes in some detail about the problems of theatrical managers: feuds between actors and managers, rivalries between managers, the debilitating results of the star system, uncooperative stock holders and the proliferation of new theatres.

414a. *Theatrical Biography; or, the Life of an Actor and Manager.* Glasgow: R. Griffin, 1848. 324 pp.

This is another edition of *Twenty-Six Years.*

Whiffin, Blanche Galton, 1845-1936.

415. *Keeping Off the Shelf.* New York: Dutton, 1928. 203 pp.

Whiffin was the daughter, sister and wife of singers, with all of whom she traveled and performed, chiefly in light opera. Whiffin was in both of the first American productions of *Pinafore* and *Hazel Kirke*. She writes of some of the changes taking place in New York theatre at the turn of the twentieth century, chiefly the move uptown. She also remembers the frontier theatres of Virginia City, Salt Lake City, Portland and San Francisco. One of the chief values of the book is found in the description of domestic life of two happily married performers who took time out to have children and often went their separate ways, without trauma or rancour, to honor individual engagements.

Wild, Sam, 1815-1883.

416. *The Original, Complete, and Only Authentic Story of "Old Wild's" (the Yorkshire "Richardson's," and the Pioneer of the Provincial Theatre): a Nursery of Strolling Players and the Celebrities who Appeared There, Being the Reminiscences of its Chief and Last Proprietor, "Sam" Wild.* Ed. "Trim," pseud of William Broadley Megson. Reprinted from the Halifax Courier. London: G. Vickers; Bradford: J. Morgan, 1888.

Wild first entered show business in the 1820s when his mother set up a traveling show known as a booth, in this case specializing in circus acts. Stimulated by the encouragement of friends, the family, plus a few strolling players, painted three backdrops in order to present plays in which the ten-year-old Sam appeared. The company continued into Wild's old age despite fires and his imprisonment for debt. In 1883, only a few months before his death, he was still appearing on stage.

Wilde, Oscar, 1854-1900.

417. *The Letters of Oscar Wilde*. Ed. Rupert Hart-Davis. London: Oxford University Press, 1962. 958 pp.

The book contains 1098 of Wilde's letters, divided according to time and place of writing, ranging from his years at Oxford (1875-1878) to the final years just after his release from Reading Gaol. He writes about the staging of his own plays and the actors and actresses who appeared in them. In these letters, which cover his entire life, he makes references to politicians such as Gladstone, controversial figures such as Dreyfus, writers such as Ernest Dowson and many theatrical figures. He has revealing comments on art and morality, censorship and bohemianism.

Williams, Bransby, 1870-1961.

418. *An Actor's Story* by Himself. London: Chapman and Hall, 1909. 270 pp.

Williams, who began his career in amateur theatricals and working-men's drama clubs, became a music hall performer, who made Dickensian characters his specialty. He has information on many music hall stars like Dan Leno and Harry Lauder and accounts of two tours of America.

419. *Bransby Williams* by Himself. With a Foreword by Naomi Jacob . . . London: Hutchinson, 1954. 240 pp.

Williams in this second memoir writes chiefly of his twentieth-century experiences. Nevertheless, he does give way to nostalgic reminiscences about his early days in the theatre in the last decade of the nineteenth century. These memories include music halls, working-men's clubs, the price of necessities, and the variety of roles he played. His disregard for chronology means that these reveries of the nineteenth century are scattered throughout the book.

Williams, Montague, 1835-1892.

420. *Leaves of a Life, Being the Reminiscences of Montague Williams*. London and New York: Macmillan and Co., 1890. Two Vols.

Williams was briefly a soldier in the Crimean War, an actor and a playwright before deciding to devote himself to law. He toured the provinces and married actress Louise Keeley. He also wrote plays in collaboration with Frank Burnand and knew the Wignans, Henry Irving, Charles Wyndham, and many others. He gives interesting accounts of the theatrical careers of his wife and her parents. Except for these brief sketches, the book is about the famous and infamous cases he knew or was involved with as a lawyer.

420a. *Leaves of a Life* . . . London and New York: Macmillan Co., 1899. 374 pp.

Wilson, Francis, 1854-1935.

421. *Francis Wilson's Life of Himself*. New York: Houghton Mifflin Co., 1924. 463 pp.

In addition to relating the events of his life and the people he knew through a career that covered large parts of the nineteenth and twentieth centuries, Wilson describes the growth of the theatrical syndicate and the clash between management and actors that led to the Actor's Equity Association. He comments on developments in the drama, on the requisite qualities of an actor and on acting schools. The book traces his own career from a general utility position with the Chestnut Street Theatre to his roles in musical plays and the writing of a highly successful play called *The Bachelor's Baby*.

422. *Recollections of a Player* by Francis Wilson. New York: De Vinne Press, 1897. 81 pp.

Wilson records his first stage appearance at the age of ten during the Civil War. He remembers the audiences of war-time soldiers, the tours and the circuses he joined. Among the famous individuals he sketches are Edwin Booth, Edwin Forrest, Walt Whitman and Joe Jefferson.

Winslow, Catherine Mary Reignolds, 1814-

423. *Yesterday With Actors.* Boston: Cupples and Hurd, 1887. 201 pp.

A nine-page autobiographical sketch opens this memoir. In these early pages, Winslow relates going on the stage at fourteen to support her parents and brothers and sisters. The rest of the volume is organized into a series of character sketches, each at some time an associate of the actress. She makes clear that she is only interested in their professional lives. Special attention is given to Charlotte Cushman, Edwin Forrest, John Brougham, Laura Keene, Agnes Robertson and E. A. Sothern.

423a. *Yesterday With Actors.* Freeport, N.Y.: Books for Libraries Press, 1972. 201 pp.

Winston, James, 1773-1843.

424. *Drury Lane Journal: Selections from James Winston's Diaries, 1819-1827.* Ed. Alfred L. Melson and Gilbert B. Cross. London: Society for Theatre Research, 1974. 162 pp.

After a brief and unsuccessful stint as an actor, James Winston turned to management--at the Olympic, then the Haymarket and, finally, Drury Lane, recording his experiences in several diaries. The only diary which is published and available is the one from 1820 to 1827, covering his years at Drury Lane. Winston is more candid about the gamier side of theatre life than are most other nineteenth-century historians. He writes of paternity suits, fist-fights, back-stage seductions, and the ever-present plague of drunkenness among performers, including one night when the entire band reported to work drunk. He records green-room entertainments, expenses of production, contracts and negotiations and his constant battle in trying to keep actors in all the parts, despite persistent illnesses, both real and feigned.

Wood, William B., 1779-1861.

425. *Old Drury Lane of Philadelphia.* Ed. Reese D. James. Philadelphia: University of Pennsylvania Press, 1932. 694 pp.

Along with a "History of the Philadelphia Stage, 1800-1832," Reese James includes the *Diary* or *Daily Account Book* which William Wood kept while co-manager of the Chestnut Street Company. Wood kept records of the dates on which plays and entertainments were presented along with the weekly receipts, and the names of players receiving benefits in each of the four theatres controlled by Warren and Wood: Alexandria, Washington, Philadelphia and Baltimore.

426. *Personal Recollections of the Stage* by William Wood. Philadelphia: H. C. Baird, 1855. 477 pp.

This American actor and manager writes of many matters concerning the American theatre in its first two decades in the nineteenth century: records of receipts for individual plays during different seasons, the "value" of certain actors, irresponsible actors, competition, a fickle public, and the effect on the theatre of fire, yellow fever, and riots. Wood ends his account with advice to young managers about the conduct of rehearsals, the use of scenic effects and the need for advertising.

426a. *Personal Recollections of the Stage*. Third Thousand. Philadelphia: H. C. Baird, 1855. 477 pp.

426b. *Personal Recollections of the Stage*. American Culture Series 46:2. Ann Arbor: University Microfilms, 1956. 477 pp.

Yates, Edmund, 1831-1894.

427. *Edmund Yates: His Recollections and Experiences*. London: Richard Bentley and Sons, 1884. Two Vols.

Yates, a journalist, novelist, playwright and son of a successful actor, Frederick Henry Yates, offers an excellent description of London life in the 1840s: he writes of eating houses, celebrities, social conditions, gambling houses, sports and the drama.

427a. *Edmund Yates . . .* Fourth Ed. With an Additional Chapter. London: Richard Bentley and Son, 1885. Two Vols.

427b. *Edmund Yates*. Another Ed. Monro, 188?. Two Vols.

427c. *Edmund Yates . . .* New York: Harper and Brothers, 1885. Two Vols.

Index of Books Discussing Theatrical Activity in Particular Theatres and Locations

The numbers below refer to item numbers in the Bibliography.

Author and Subject Index

The numbers below refer to item numbers in the Bibliography.

About the Compilers

CLAUDIA D. JOHNSON is Associate Professor and Chairperson of the Department of English at the University of Alabama, Tuscaloosa. She has published extensively on nineteenth-century English and American literature and theatre. Her works include *The Productive Tension of Hawthorne's Art*, *An Annotated Bibliography of Shakespearean Burlesques and Travesties*, *Perspective on America: The Nineteenth-Century American Actress*, and articles in *American Literature*, *American Quarterly*, and *Theatre Survey*.

VERNON E. JOHNSON is a retired professor of Dramatic Literature with twenty-five years' experience as an actor and director in professional and academic theatre.